D1083873

05/01/2023

Dr. Suzan Johnson Cook

From Me
To You . . . Enjoy!

Deidra Roberts

mascotbooks.com

From Me to You: The Power of Storytelling and Its Inherent Generational Wealth— An African American Story

©2022 Deidra R. Moore-Janvier. All Rights Reserved. No part of this publication may be reproduced, stored in a retrieval system or transmitted in any form by any means electronic, mechanical, or photocopying, recording or otherwise without the permission of the author.

Although the author and publisher have made every effort to ensure that the information in this book was correct at press time, the author and publisher do not assume and hereby disclaim any liability to any party for any loss, damage, or disruption caused by errors or omissions, whether such errors or omissions result from negligence, accident, or any other cause.

Excerpts from the book *Marcus Garvey, Hero: A First Biography, Vol 1* by Anthony Martin. Courtesy of The Majority Press.

Excerpts from the book *For Freedom's Sake: The Life of Fannie Lou Hamer* by Kai Lee. Courtesy of University of Illinois Press.

Requests for speaking events, extra book copies, or permissions should be addressed to dmoore2253@gmail.com.

For more information, please contact:
Mascot Books
620 Herndon Parkway #320
Herndon, VA 20170
info@mascotbooks.com

CPSIA Code: PRV0122A
Library of Congress Control Number: 2021912817
ISBN-13: 978-1-64543-623-2

Printed in the United States

To the Storytellers of My Legacy

- The tens of millions of African lives lost during the transatlantic slave trade and the other slave trades that existed throughout time

- Toussaint L'ouverture—the Haitian (Afro-Caribbean) leader who fought and made significant contributions to the establishment of the first Black nation in 1804, the nation first to abolish slavery

- The tens of thousands of African American lives lost during both the American Revolutionary War and the American Civil War

- The tens of thousands of African American lives lost during the Reconstruction era, the era of Jim Crow laws, and the Civil Rights movement

- The tens of thousands of abolitionists, freedom fighters, and other courageous people who fought on the battlefield of life to make our America a place to live with civil rights for all!

"We must not see any person as an abstraction. Instead, we must see in every person a universe with its own secrets, with its own treasures, with its own sources of anguish, and with some measure of triumph."

—Elie Wiesel

From Me To You

The Power of Storytelling and Its Inherent Generational Wealth—

An African American Story

Story by

Deidra R. Moore-Janvier, Esq.

Illustrated by
Valerie Bouthyette

Prelude

"If there is a book that you want to read, but it hasn't been written yet, then you must write it."

—Toni Morrison

Hello,

I wanted to share with you a special project that I have been working on since September 2019. It was about one week after our son, Justin, turned eight years old that he had the opportunity to visit a nursing home, where he met and spoke with one of the last remaining Holocaust survivors. The trip was a part of the Service Learning Club at his school.

The Service Learning Club is a program that helps to develop a sense of community in the children as they develop their minds and build their character throughout the school year. The Service Learning Club teaches children to "reflect on the needs of the community and guides children to consider tangible ways to make a positive difference in the lives of others."

This trip led to one of Justin's friends sharing stories about the Holocaust—as told to him by his own family. Surprisingly, the discussion between my eight-year-old son and his nine-year-old friend allowed them to make a connection between the events of the Holocaust in Germany and the events of slavery in America.

That night, while talking about our day, Justin shared the conversation he had with his peer about the Holocaust. Justin then asked the difficult question, "What is slavery?"

When asked this question, I was taken aback. I thought, *It's just too soon. He only turned eight years old a week ago!* After thinking through how best to make this a "teachable moment" for Justin and others, I decided to put pen to paper and began researching and writing this book. I wanted to, in the most thoughtful and purposeful way possible, share that part of our history—slavery and the African American experience.

So here goes—this is *From Me to You!*

Contents

Introduction

This book, *From Me to You: The Power of Storytelling and Its Inherent Generational Wealth—An African American Story*, was born out of love for my children. It is right on time for my son, who is a minor, but my daughter might argue that it is a bit too late for her, as she is an adult now. My response to her would be, "It is never too late to learn about your history." Besides, you can't know where you are going unless you know where you came from, and since we are all still becoming who we are, time is not lost on anyone!

Purpose

"Nothing in life is to be feared, it is only to be understood. Now is the time to understand more, so that we may fear less."

—Marie Curie

I wrote this book simply because I needed to find a way to talk to my eight-year-old son about the difficult topics surrounding slavery and racism—particularly racism in America. And to me, an African American mother, wife, and citizen of the United States, you can't talk about one without addressing the other.

The problem, as I see it, is that people are quick to dismiss the notion that racism still exists in America and are just as quick to say, "Ah, just leave it alone. Slavery happened so long ago!" Therein lies the problem. People want to brush slavery off as being a "thing of the past." But how do you get over the effects of slavery and racism in America when we are not willing to get uncomfortable enough to have a discussion about the topic, its origin, and the devastating impact it had, and continues to have, upon an entire race of people?

Now that my eight-year-old son has been showing awareness of the topic and has asked the question, "What is slavery?" I am compelled to sit down and delve deeper into the subject. It is clear that the time is now! So there began my gathering, from our home library, of books that spoke to various aspects of slavery and/or racism in America. The challenge for me was finding that one book that told the story surrounding slavery in a thoughtful, compassionate, yet direct, rich, and undistorted manner.

I have not found the one book that has been able to hit all the chords: what to say and how to say it—specifically in a way that covers those historical moments that are so intimately intertwined with American history—topics such as: the transatlantic slave trade; the Middle Passage; the African diaspora; the Resistance and the Resilience; the American Civil War; the Reconstruction era; Black Code laws; Jim Crow laws; Civil Rights Movement; and of course, leading up through the election of the first African American president of the United States of America.

Quoting Civil Rights leader John Lewis, "The scars and stains of racism are still deeply embedded in the American society." Our children must know that the colonial times, particularly that time leading up to the creation of the "New World" and ultimately America, was a time when America was founded upon a "racial caste system." White people in this New World structure were to be the management and wealth holders (the upper class); and the black people from Africa were to be the laborers (the underclass). "This racial caste system afforded white people the opportunity to secure wealth and power—by exploiting the labor and lives of our ancestors, the enslaved Africans. This endeavor of the forefathers was sanctioned within the government structure that was formed during the creation of our imperfect nation, the United States of America."

Our children must know that racial inequality in America has not only impacted the lives of African Americans, but also people such as Asian Americans, Latin Americans, Jewish Americans, Native Americans, and other groups.

They must recognize that issues like systemic racism, economic inequality, and achievement gaps are the results of man-made policies in America. They must also recognize that stereotypes perpetuated by others have nothing to do with their ability to learn, to analyze, to think critically, to ask questions, or to make constructive arguments. This is especially important as they learn to navigate this thing called life.

The responsibility is on us and the generations to come to remember these historical moments and honor the mandate that comes with them.

The goal of this book is to enlighten those who are unwilling, afraid, unaware, or just unsure of where to start engaging their young children on the subject of the institution of slavery and many other historical atrocities upon mankind. My hope is that you will find this book to be somewhat of a blueprint for starting, continuing, memorializing, and sharing the conversation about slavery, particularly as it relates to American history!

I recalled what a dear friend, Edwidge Danticat, stated (quoting Toni Morrison during a visit to my son's school in September 2019): "If there is a book that you want to read, but it hasn't been written yet, then you must write it!"

Hence the birth of this book: *From Me to You: The Power of Storytelling and Its Inherent Generational Wealth—An African American Story!*

"Philosophers have long conceded, however, that every man has two educators: that which is given to him, and the other that which he gives himself. Of the two kinds, the latter is by far the more desirable. Indeed all that is most worthy in man he must work out and conquer for himself. It is that which constitutes our real and best nourishment. What we are merely taught seldom nourishes the mind like that which we teach ourselves."

— Carter G. Woodson
(The Father of Black History Month)

NOTABLE MENTIONS:

Carter G. Woodson was a historian and author.

After graduating from the University of Chicago, he became the second African American to earn a doctorate degree from Harvard University (the first being W.E.B. DuBois).

- In 1915, he founded the Association for the Study of African American Life and History.
- He called for a "study of the past that would be free from prejudice."
- He wrote, "The aim of this organization is to set forth facts in scientific form, for facts properly set forth will tell their own story."
- In 1926, he went on to launch African American History Week, which was expanded to Black History Month in 1976.
- He was a professor and dean at Howard University and West Virginia Collegiate Institute.
- He wrote more than thirty books, including *The Miseducation of the Negro*.

Just as the legendary Carter G. Woodson once acknowledged, he chose the month of February to launch African American History Week because Abraham Lincoln's and George Washington's birthdays are in February. I was inspired to write this book in honor of Black History Month!

You are beautiful.

You are loved.

You have civil rights.

Your life does matter.

Racism is not your burden to carry.

YOU ARE NOT THE ROOT CAUSE OF OTHER PEOPLE'S IGNORANCE, INSECURITIES, AND STEREOTYPES.

There are more good people in the world than there are bad.

You have complete control over only one thing in the universe—your thinking!

"ONE OF THE LESSONS THAT I GREW UP WITH WAS TO ALWAYS STAY TRUE TO YOURSELF AND NEVER LET WHAT SOMEBODY ELSE SAYS DISTRACT YOU FROM YOUR GOALS."

- MICHELLE OBAMA

"Knowing is not enough; we must apply. Wishing is not enough; we must do."

- Johann Wolfgang Von Goethe

Always remember: make your life a masterpiece; imagine no limitations on what you can be, have, or do.

"The way to get started is to quit talking and begin doing."

- Walt Disney

Chapter 1
The Question

*"Learn from yesterday, live for today, hope for tomorrow.
The important thing is not to stop questioning."*

—Albert Einstein

t was approximately one week after Justin turned eight years old when he asked, "Mom, what is slavery?" He continued, "Why were black people called 'colored'? Besides, black isn't a skin color—just like white isn't a skin color."

He went on to say that shades of brown, from light to dark, are possible skin colors, but not black and white. Then Justin asked, "Aren't you supposed to do what Dr. Martin Luther King, Jr. said, which is to judge people by the content of their character, not by the color of their skin?"

I looked down at this nearly fifty-four-inch-tall child and said—with a look of bewilderment upon my face—"Where do you come up with this stuff? You're only eight."

He said, with a smile upon his face that could melt butter, "I get it from you, Mom. Besides, remember the 'shoebox' project I did in second grade? The project I did about Dr. Martin Luther King, Jr.—remember, Mom?"

Before I could even gather my internal self and begin to wrap my head around the idea of talking to Justin about slavery, he hit me with another statement. "Mom, me and Zack were talking, and he was telling me about his family history surrounding the Holocaust and how the Germans treated so many of the Jewish people badly!" He continued, "Mom, what was that about? Why did Hitler do that to the Jewish people? He must have been crazy, right?"

My initial response was, *Oh my Lord. Where do I begin to discuss something so painful and incomprehensible, like the topics of slavery and the Holocaust—to my eight-year-old, nonetheless? How do you discuss "slavery" and "racism in America" to a child? Where do you start?*

Then, it dawned on me that it is crucial to his very existence in this world, particularly while living here in America, that he know the full story about the African American experience: the sacrifices, the struggles, and the empowering moments.

I wanted to be able to communicate the story of slavery, and the African American experience, in the most thoughtful and purposeful way. I did what I do best, which was to speak generally and take the necessary time to come up with the best way to communicate this very sensitive and difficult topic to my son.

Justin and I went to our bedroom. He jumped on the bed and landed across my shin. Ouch! He started to get comfortable, asking those questions again. But how to explain such an important topic in a child-appropriate way?

By the following afternoon, I had figured out a way to bring the past to life for Justin.

MOM: Come, my love, let's go on a little journey.

JUSTIN: To where, Mom?

MOM: Let's take a trip around the world.

17

MOM: All we will need are our cozy blankets,
our pillows, the world map over there,
and our book of pictures showing
the Country Spotlights that
were created in school.

CHAPTER 2

The Journey

*"If you're walking down the right path and
you're willing to keep walking, eventually
you'll make progress."*

—Barack Obama

n just a few minutes, we'd made our way to the backyard
and settled into the hammock with everything we gathered from the house.

JUSTIN: Now what, Mom?

MOM: Before I tell you about slavery and attempt to answer all the great questions you have posed, let me put things in proper context for you.

I picked up the world map and showed it to Justin.

MOM: Justin, do you know what this is?

JUSTIN: Yeah—it's a map of the different continents in the world.

MOM: How many continents are there?

JUSTIN: Seven!

MOM: Can you name the seven continents?

THE CONTINENTS

North America

South America

OF THE WORLD

Europe

Asia

Africa

Australia

Antarctica

MOM: Very good! What two bodies of water lay between North America and South America?

JUSTIN: The Caribbean Sea and the Gulf of Mexico.

JUSTIN: Daddy, look! That's the Caribbean—where Haiti is located.

DAD: Right, son. I am from Haiti. It's an island located in the Caribbean Sea. The island was originally called Hispaniola, but it was later named Haiti.

MOM: Dad was born in Haiti, but his ancestors are from the continent of Africa.

DAD: So that makes me an Afro-Caribbean.

MOM: Do you know which continent I was born on?

JUSTIN: Yes. You were born here in North America. In the United States of America.

MOM: That's correct, son. But my ancestors were also from the continent of Africa, which makes me an African American.

JUSTIN: I know, I know. And that makes me African American too, right?

MOM & DAD: *Yes!*

MOM: Justin, are there any other children in your school that you know of who are from the continent of Africa?

JUSTIN: That's a silly question. They all live here in North America. I don't know where everyone is from—all I know is that they all live here in the United States, which is where I live, Mom.

Well, except for:

- Zack, his family is from Israel;

- William, Conner, and Delia's family is from Korea;

- Alexis—well, there are two Alexises, and they are both in my class and are both from Turkey;

- Sylvia is from China;

- Stephen's family is from Southeast Asia;

- Ms. Gina, my kindergarten teacher, is from India;

- Gregory and his sister, Claire—their family is from Jamaica or somewhere in the Caribbean;

- Anna's and Warren's families are from the Dominican Republic;

- Kevin and Nicole's parents are from Puerto Rico;

- David's and Oliver's families are from England;

- Soléh's family is from Senegal;

- Jaime's and Richard's families are from Vietnam;

- And there is me, Justin, whose dad is from Haiti.

JUSTIN: We are from Africa—just like everyone is from somewhere in the world!

MOM: Hey, here is an interesting fact. Turkey is located on two continents: Asia and Europe! Look here—97 percent of the country is located in Anatolia, Western Asia, and the other region on the Balkan Peninsula is in Southeast Europe.

JUSTIN: I didn't know that! I'll check with both Defne and Asli tomorrow and see if that's accurate.

MOM: What am I going to do with you?

JUSTIN: Just love me.

MOM: Wow! There are so many people at your school whose families are from all across the world. There are families from Canada, India, Puerto Rico, Vietnam, China, Israel, Nigeria, Haiti, Dominican Republic, England, Jamaica, Senegal, Ghana, Antiqua, and Guyana, just to name a few.

TURKEY

MOM: Look at these Country Spotlights that were done in your school during the past several months. I love looking at them because it reminds everyone about the multiculturalism that exists at the school you attend.

Do you know how the Country Spotlights program started at your school?

Well, there was a mother who wanted to celebrate the diverse nature of the student body at the school. She came up with the idea of spotlighting a country once a month in the following manner:

- Wall displays in the Early Learning Building and in the Upper Learning Building, which includes the cafeteria.

- Slideshows—twenty slides—that include pictures of families, students, and/or faculty who are from or have visited the country being spotlighted; the twenty slides are shown on flat-screen TVs located outside the gym and the cafeteria.

- A book list that shares titles of culturally relevant books for consideration.

- Special Menu Day in which parents volunteer and coordinate with the school lunch personnel to arrange hot lunch items that are authentic to the country being recognized.
- Music from the country being featured to be played during the morning runs.

SPOTLIGHT - CANADA

HOLIDAY / Boxing Day, December 26th.
CAFETERIA MENU on Dec 11th / French Pea Soup, Baked Yukon Fries, Poutine, Maple Syrup Glazed Brussels Sprouts, Smoked Beef Sandwiches, Roasted Chicken, Butter Tarts
MUSIC / Justin Bieber, Shawn Mendes, and Avril Lavigne

Special Lunch Menu

Early Learning Display

Books

Slideshow

Canada's Four Seasons!

Upper Learning Display

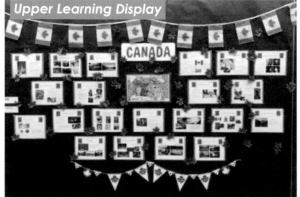

Cafeteria Display

CHINA

SPECIAL LUNCH DISHES/
Egg Drop Soup, Steamed
Chicken Dumplings, Steamed
Vegetarian Kale Dumplings,
White Rice, Mango Pudding

MORNING RUN MUSIC /
Manual of Youth by TFboys,
Big Fish & Begonia theme song,
The Butterfly Lovers Violin
Concerto

EL BUILDING

ON DISPLAY
TIL MAY 31st

SLIDESHOW

BOOKS

UL HALLWAY

CAFETERIA

Below: Chef Dave puts
the final touch on the
Mango Pudding served
on May 15th for the
China Special Menu Day!

SPOTLIGHT - INDIA

FESTIVAL / Diwali began October 27th, the LS celebrated on November 6

CAFETERIA MENU / Makai Ka Shorba (Corn Soup), Lemon Rice, Daal (Lentil Curry), Paalak Paneer (Spinach and Cheese), and Mango Lassi on November 8

Upper Learning Displays

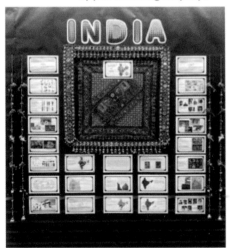

Diwali Menu

Cafeteria Display

Ask A Spotlight Question! A great addition to the monthly spotlights have been the question boxes located besdie the EL and UL displays. Students can ask anything related to the country or celebration of the month. We have already received *"Is Diwali the only Indian Holiday?"* and *"Does Diwali have a certain amount of days?"* amongst other questions so it is great to hear the displays are sparking further interest in the students! Please encourage your children to ask a question and we are happy to get the answers to them!

MONTHLY
SPOTLIGHT
Created by parent volunteers with an authentic view

IPC

SPOTLIGHT/NOV/ENGLAND**/JAN/**RUSSIA**/FEB/**NIGERIA**/MAR/**ISRAEL**/MAY/**CHINA

NIGERIA

UL BUILING

 On display till Feb. 28th

BOOKS

WHY THE SKY IS FAR AWAY
A NIGERIAN FOLKTALE

Why Mosquitoes Buzz in People's Ears
Verna Aardema
pictures by Leo and Diane Dillon

EXPLORING WORLD CULTURES
Nigeria

EXPLORING COUNTRIES
Nigeria

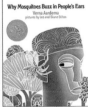

SLIDESHOW

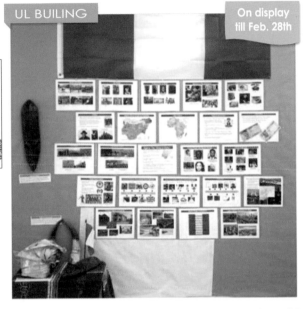

FESTIVAL Calabar Carnival **DATE** December –31
LS CAFETERIA DISHES FEB. 37 Nigerian Jollof
Rice with Chicken and Fried Pantains

MORNING RUN MUSIC/ Fall by Davido,
Lady by Fela Kuti, Final by Wizkid, Sekem
by Mc Galaxy

UL HALLWAY

NIGERIA

CAFETERIA

SPOTLIGHT - SENEGAL

Early Learning Display

Special Thanks to POC for leading this spotlight! On display till Feb 27th

Slideshow

SENEGAL

Baobab tree: The nation's symbol, and can be found throughout much of sub-Saharan Africa.

It's elements (like the baobab fruit and leaves) are nutritional and beneficial.

Cafeteria Display

Upper Learning Display

SENEGAL

CELEBRATION / Black History Month
DATE / Feb 1st through Feb 29th

CAFETERIA MENU FEB 12 / Root Vegetable Soup, Poulet Yassa (Senegalese Chicken), White Rice, Green Peas

MUSIC / Youssou Ndour, Estelle and Akon

Special Lunch Menu

Books

Waali le petit Talibe

La fête du mouton

46

SPOTLIGHT-VIETNAM

Festival/ Lunar New Year begins January 25th.
CAFETERIA MENU on Jan 15th/ Pho Soup, Lemongrass Chicken, Vietnamese Noodles, Sticky White Rice, Steamed Pork Buns, Vegetable Spring Rolls.
MUSIC/ Hoang Thuy Linh, Pixel Neko.

Slideshow

Early Learning Display

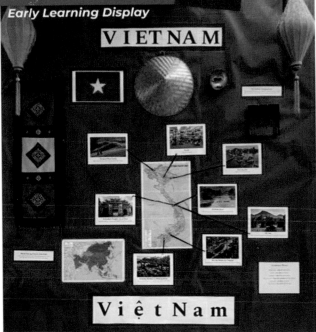

Upper Learning Display

Books

Special Lunch Menu

HAITI

LUNCH DISHES APRIL 17th /
Joumon Soup (Pumpkin Soup)
Haitian Patties and KoKonet
(Coconut) cookies

THANKS TO / Deidra
Moore-Janvier & Pierre Janvier.

EL BUILDING

UL HALLWAY

CAFETERIA

BOOKS

The Moore-Janvier
family with author
Edwidge Danticat of
*Eight Days:
A Story of Haiti*

MONTHLY
SPOTLIGHT

Created by parent volunteers with an authentic view

 ISRAEL

EL BUILDING

SPECIAL LUNCH DISHES/
Matzo Ball Soup, Labneh, Roasted Eggplant Matbucha, Israeli Salad, Israeli Corn Salad, Hummus, Chicken Shawarma, Israeli Rice Pilaf, Pita Bread.

MORNING RUN MUSIC/
Barbie by Satic & Ben El, Mesiba BeHaifa by The Ultras, Tazizu by Eden Ben Zaken.

SLIDESHOW

ISRAEL

UL HALLWAY

CAFETERIA

BETEAVON!
(beh-tay-ah-vohn)
Hebrew for "Good Appetite!"
בְּתֵאָבוֹן!

BOOKS

Everybody Says Shalom

Flag by Shira

A YOM HA'ATZMAUT S...

SUDDENLY A KNOCK ON THE DOOR
ETGAR KERET

NEW YORK TIMES BESTSELLER

MY PROMISED LAND
ARI SHAVIT
THE TRIUMPH AND TRAGEDY OF ISRAEL

JUSTIN: Yeah, Mom, I remember when we did the Haiti Country Spotlight. It was cool! But what does this have to do with slavery and why people are called "colored"?

MOM: Well, Justin, those are great questions. But hold on, we're getting there! Remember, this is a journey, not a race. It's a lot to take in, and I want to make sure that you understand all that surrounds this very difficult yet empowering story surrounding the history of our culture—the African American culture. It will be quite a journey, over many years and many continents, and involve many people…

CHAPTER 3
Beginnings

"Children must be taught how to think, not what to think."

—Margaret Mead

"Awareness is all about restoring your freedom to choose what you want, instead of what your past imposes on you."

—Deepak Chopra

"So you want to know what slavery is—or was, right?" asked Mom.

"Yep," Justin replied.

"Why don't you share with me your definition of slavery?"

"Okay! Well, what is slavery? Hmm." Justin lay inside the hammock with his finger on his head. Then he said, "So, you have Black people and white farmers or landowners. Say they [the landowners] want you [the Black people] to work for them. Simple, right?"

He continued, "But instead of treating you like actual human beings, they treat you like farm tools."

"Farm tools?" Mom asked. "What do you mean they treat you like farm tools?"

Justin replied, "Well, you know—they treat you like farm tools because of the color of your skin."

Mom looked puzzled. "Tell me more."

They sat upright on the hammock. Justin's eyes searched the yard. "It's like that rake over there."

"What about that rake makes you think of slavery?"

Justin jumped off the hammock, leaving it—and Mom—swinging behind him.

Justin grabbed the rake and started raking the few leaves that had fallen in the yard.

"You see, Mom, this rake is a special kind of tool. Right?"

"Right!"

"You use it for its intended purpose, right?

"Yep!"

"And its intended purpose is to rake the leaves on the ground. So, Mom, look. If this is your rake, and you or Daddy did not want it anymore, you could easily get rid of it.

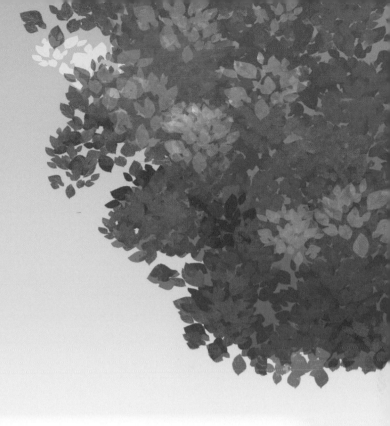

"But you can also just trade it with, let's say our neighbor, right?"

"Right again," Mom said.

"Well, what I mean is they—the white farmer or landowner—could trade or sell them."

"Trade or sell what? The farm tools?"

"No, Mom. The Black people. They could trade and sell the Black people."

"Oh, now I see. So slavery to you is a time in our history when Black people were treated like objects?"

"Yes, that is exactly what I mean."

"You know, that's a pretty good description of what slavery means. Now go ask Dad what his definition of slavery is, and let's see what he says."

"Hey, Dad," Justin began, "what's your definition of slavery?"

Dad stood nearby, watering the trees with the hose. "Well, son, I don't really have a separate definition from the norm, but let's see … it is forced labor, indentured servitude; it is like being a prisoner. You are made to work under the most difficult conditions. For example, long hours under the sun in scantily-clad clothing."

Dad continued, "I don't have a classical definition, but it is almost like imprisonment. The slaves could not travel freely; they could not move about without being accounted for every minute of the day."

"What are forced labor and indentured servitude?" asked Justin.

"They are terms that's used to describe circumstances under which people are made to work without being paid to do the work."

Just then, Justin's sister, Sis, entered the yard to join the family. She made her way toward the tree she knew Justin liked to sit in.

Sis chimed in, "Well, slavery means the act of working with no pay—or it sounds like doing a lot of things for work but being underpaid, if paid at all."

Justin ran over to Mom, who was trying to steady the hammock. He climbed on and lay next to her. Justin looked up at Mom and asked, "So now what exactly is slavery, Mom?"

Mom looked down at Justin and replied, "Well, my love, the institution of slavery is complex. You see, not all slaves that have existed in places like Europe, China, Korea, Japan, India, Spain, Greece, and other parts of the world were treated as brutally, inhumanely, and unjustly as African slaves came to be treated, particularly during the development of the transatlantic slave trade starting around the 1500s.

"Consequently, I will say slavery can be broadly defined as the ownership, buying, and selling of human beings for the purpose of forced and unpaid labor."

Let's look at some terms that you will come across:

"DURESS" means:
- constraint illegally exercised to force someone to perform an act; for example, forcible restraint or imprisonment.

"SLAVERY" means:
- an institution wherein a person is legally owned by others and forced to work for them.

A **"SLAVE"** is:
- a human being, under circumstances involving duress, who was considered to be the property of another person.

An **"ENSLAVED PERSON"** is:
- a human being who, under duress, was made to be a slave, to be bought and sold.

"INDENTURED SERVITUDE" is:
- the act of working or providing services or labor for little or no pay.

"CHATTEL SLAVERY" is:
- a specific servitude relationship where the slave is treated as the property of the owner.[1] As such, the owner is free to sell, trade, or treat the slave as he would other pieces of property, and the children of the slave often are retained as the property of the master.[2]

"So, Mom," Justin said, "when did slavery start? Where did it happen? Who was affected by it? How was it created? And why did it exist?

"And Mom, why did they refer to people as 'colored' or 'Black' or even 'white'? I know that when those terms are used, they are used in a way to describe the color of one's skin, but those are not even skin colors. For example, Mom, listen, my skin color is not black—no one's skin color is black. Look at Uncle William; his skin color is not white. It's actually like a beige-ish color with freckles. My point is, Mom, that I don't know why they call our ancestors colored people, when

black is not an actual skin color, just like white is not an actual skin color. Why were Black people referred to as colored? What do people who use those references think—do they think people are like crayons and you can just color them in whatever color you want to? It just doesn't make any sense."

Mom responded, "Well, my dear, that's another long story, but I will say this: yes, there are different shades of skin tones that we each carry, ranging from dark brown to light brown, from light brown to a fair skin tone. Technically, you are right—the skin tones of people are neither 'black' nor 'white' in its true color form. These were concepts that are used, particularly in America, to separate the races.

"The terms 'colored people' and 'black people' were used as a way to describe one's ethnicity. Historically, African Americans have been referred to by racial pejoratives (words or

phrases that have negative connotations and are used to disparage or belittle a person) during different points in time—racial pejoratives such as 'Negroes' and 'colored' or 'colored people.'

"As you will learn, it was a painstaking fight to get to the point where we are now referred to as African Americans, an ethnic group born in America but whose ancestors are direct descendants of the motherland/continent of Africa.

"And Justin, those are great questions you asked," Mom said. "But hold on, hold on—we are getting there. Remember, this is a journey, not a race.

"It's a lot to take in, and I want to make sure that you understand all that is involved in this very difficult story surrounding the topic of "What is slavery?" and, more importantly, "What is the history of slavery?" which is an integral part of our, the African American, culture.

"For many years, the history of African Americans was not often told in books or in school. Back in the day, some people would rely on family stories, handed down from generation to generation. Otherwise, you might have to do a bit of detective work to find out anything at all about this facet of our nation's history—poring over historical records and looking through books and photos. In fact, this is the process I undertook way back when, when Sis was around ten years old and your great-grandmother was alive. I recall spending time at the Schomberg Library in Harlem, conducting research on our family history. I needed to do that for myself as much as I needed to do it for Sis; but that's another story for another day—sorry, I digress.

"The point is that the lack of available information about our culture led to the spread of false or misleading stories about the culture and experiences of the enslaved Africans and their descendants. These stories are called myths or stereotypes.

A "**MYTH**" is:

- any invented story, idea, or concept
- an imaginary or fictitious thing or person
- an unproved or false collective belief that is used to justify a social institution

A "**STEREOTYPE**" is:

- a set idea that people have about what someone or something is like, especially an idea that is wrong.

Many myths, prejudices, untruths, and misunderstandings about enslaved Africans and their descendants spread and continue to exist all over the world, including in our own imperfect country, the United States of America. Whether it is depicting African Americans in the news media, in schoolbooks, on television shows, in movies, on employment applications, in the classrooms, in the boardrooms, in the workplace, and many other outlets as being criminals, unintelligent, nonfamily orientated, barbarian or the like, false narratives have been placed upon Africans and their descendants for centuries. This rhetoric can only serve one purpose that is, to depict us in the light most favorable to justify the institution of slavery and the resulting brutality, oppressive treatment, and millions of lives lost. The goal is also to do so with practicably no accountability as for the impact it would have upon the more than twenty generations that would follow slavery.

"As you grow older, you will hear a lot of myths and stereotypes about the African American culture. And as you grow wiser, always know that just because someone says it's so does not mean it is! Always research, investigate a situation beyond that which you see or hear on the surface, and, my love, always go deeper to ensure a full, undistorted understanding of everything!

"In our discussions, you will hear concepts, terms, and references relating to those historical moments which have adversely affected and thus have had a horrible and devastating impact upon the lives of the enslaved Africans and their descendants for more than 146,365 days. Some you have heard during this current time—things like the Arab slave trade, the transatlantic slave trade, abolitionists, Emancipation, the American Civil War, the Reconstruction era, black codes, the Jim Crow laws, the Civil Rights era, and racism and discrimination. Whenever you have questions about any of the topics you will learn in this book, don't hesitate to come to me, Dad, Sis, Tatie, or a teacher or administrator whom you feel you can have an honest conversation with about the subject of slavery.

"And don't be afraid to use the skill sets you are developing at school, like the ability to think critically, ask questions, and make constructive arguments. Okay!" Mom finished.

Justin replied, "Okay, Mom. I won't forget!"

Chapter 4

Into the Past

"Ignorance or concealment of major historical events constitutes an obstacle to mutual understanding."

—UNESCO mandate

"Well, Justin," said Mom, "the answer to the question 'What is the history of slavery?' will vary depending upon whom the question is presented to. For example, some folks might say:

- Slavery began about 401 years ago (1619), when Africans were forced to emigrate from their home country on the African continent, were transported to the Americas, especially North America, and scattered throughout the Virginia colony.

Others might say:

- Slavery started in Africa when Africans were enslaving other Africans, thousands of years before the arrival of the Europeans.

No matter what definitions you may come across in life surrounding slavery, you need to know the following facts about Africa, the enslaved Africans and their descendants, and about the institution of slavery:

i. Our history does not start and end with slavery.

ii. Slavery, while a crucial part of American history, does not define who we are as a people.

iii. Always remember that our ancestors—particularly the enslaved Africans and their descendants, those who were extricated from their homeland of Africa, dispersed throughout the world, and placed into forced labor (helping to develop wealth, power, and empires for other nations, and doing so under the most egregious, brutal, and inhumane conditions) were an amazing and phenomenal group of peoples notwithstanding. Yet still we rise! Always know this!

iv. Always remember that our ancestors originated from the beautiful continent of Africa, a continent surrounded by three massive and beautiful bodies of water:

» the *Mediterranean Sea* on the Northern part of the continent, which lies between Europe and Asia;

» the *Atlantic Ocean* on the western part of the continent (situated across from the North and South Americas in the western hemisphere);

» the *Indian Ocean* on the eastern and southeastern part of the continent, situated across from Australia and parts of Asia.

v.   Africa is a continent through which the longest river in the world flows—the beautiful Nile River, a.k.a. the River Nile.

vi.   Always remember that our ancestors originated from a continent diverse in people, climate, language, wildlife, religion, and culture and continent rich in minerals, tropical fruits, precious metals and with an abundance of natural resources found throughout the continent, such as petroleum products, natural gas, uranium, copper, cotton, rubber, crude oil, textiles, fish, timber, diamonds, coffee, tea, grains, livestock, oil, and tobacco, just to name a few!

vii.   Always know that the enslaved Africans and their descendants did not willingly participate in the institution of slavery, in America or elsewhere.

viii.   Remember that Africans were not the first, nor the only ethnic group, subjected to slavery.

ix.   Know that there are other ethnic groups that have a history involving the enslavement of their people. For example, Jewish people; Italian people; Chinese, Korean, and Japanese people; Arabs and people from the Middle East; Indigenous Americans; Irish people; Dutch people (from the Netherlands); Spanish people; Brazilians; Turkish people from Eastern Europe; people from parts of India; and many other ethnic groups around the world have a shared history surrounding some form of slavery.

x.   Historically, the enslavement of people has occurred in many ways. For example, a person can be enslaved:

- » as *punishment for a crime*;

- » as *repayment of a debt*—where a person owes a debt to another; the debtor (the person who created the debt) would pledge their services as security, as the repayment of the debt;

- » as a *prisoner of war*—a person is captured during or immediately after an armed conflict, and now asserts control over you; one's release could be ransomed or negotiated under certain circumstances;

- » as a *child born to enslaved mothers*;

- » *voluntarily* (that is, to escape starvation in times of famine as was done in ancient India); and apparently,

- » by being *snatched up, kidnapped, forcibly removed from your homeland, and dispersed throughout the world*; and

- » via the form of *chattel slavery*, where the person is treated as the private property of another, to be bought and sold at the owner's will.

It is important that you know slavery was practiced in ancient civilization, the Middle Ages, and more modern times. People of different religions and cultures have practiced and accepted slavery at some point in time: Christianity, Islam, Buddhism, Catholicism, and Judaism.

In all periods of the existence of the Roman Empire, it is well known that the Roman economy was based on slavery. But one notable aspect of slavery during that time was that slavery, for the most part, was not based on one's skin color or race. In fact, during the Roman Empire and into the early Middle Ages, there were enslaved Europeans, which consisted of the white race, found in every region of the subcontinent. The Roman Empire used the form of chattel slavery for labor—using the slaves as private property.

During the period of the Islamic Empire (seventh to twentieth century), Muslims were known to have used slaves to build their economy. In fact, during the ninth century, "exports of slaves to the Muslim world from across the Sahara Desert and across the Indian Ocean began after Muslim Arab and Swahili traders won control of the Swahili Coast and sea routes. These traders captured Bantu peoples (Zanj) from the interior in the present-day lands of Kenya, Mozambique, and Tanzania and brought them to the coast."[3,4] Moreover, "Muslim merchants traded an estimated one thousand African slaves annually between the years 800 and 1700, a number that grew to four thousand during the eighteenth century and 3,700 during the period from 1800 to 1870."

During the period of the Ottoman Empire (1299 to 1923), slavery was a legal and significant part of its economy and traditional society. The main source of slaves were wars and politically organized enslavement expeditions in North and East Africa, Eastern Europe, the Balkans, and the Caucasus.[5]

Lastly, during the Portuguese Empire (1415–1580), Portugal also established its economy and wealth and maintained its empire with the extensive use of slavery.

Likewise, it is well known that Spain established its economy and wealth through the widespread use of slavery. In fact:

When the Spaniards conquered the New World, they resorted to a system of forced labor called the encomienda. An encomienda was an organization in which a Spaniard received a restricted set of property rights over Indian labor from the Crown whereby the Spaniard (an encomendero) could extract tribute (payment of a portion of output) from the Indians in the form of goods, metals, money, or direct labor services.

In exchange, encomenderos provided the Indians protection and instruction in the Catholic faith, promised to defend the area, and paid a tax to the Crown.

Property rights over Indian labor were restricted in three ways. First, Indians were not owned by encomenderos; they could not be bought, sold, or rented to others. Second, encomenderos were forbidden inheritance rights. Encomenderos did not automatically transfer to future generations. They would revert to the Crown upon the death of the second generation encomendero, to be kept by the Crown or given to another Spaniard. Third, Indians could not be relocated from their proximate geographical area. The encomenderos were only given a right to the labor, not the land. These restrictions on trading, inheritance, and relocation distinguished Indians in encomiendas from slaves.[6]

As for slavery in Africa, even before the arrival of the Europeans on the continent of Africa, some regions had their own system of slavery. Africans were enslaved—as a punishment for a crime, payment for a debt, or as a prisoner of war. However, the form of chattel slavery would be realized again through European invasion and will prove to be completely different from the form that existed in Africa.

Slavery was a part of the economic structure of African societies for many centuries, although the extent varied.[7,8] Ibn Battuta, who visited the ancient kingdom of Mali in the mid-fourteenth century, recounts that the local inhabitants vied with each other in the number of slaves and servants they had, and was himself given a slave boy as a "hospitality gift."[9] In sub-Saharan Africa, the slave relationships were often complex, with rights and freedoms given to individuals held in slavery and restrictions on sale and treatment by their masters.[10] Many communities had hierarchies between different types of slaves: for example, differentiating between those who had been born into slavery and those who had been captured through war.[11]

The concept and practice of slavery has played a major role in aspects of different religions, such as Christianity, Islam, Buddhism, and Judaism.

In fact, slavery has been a part of the Islamic world for the past 1,300 years, after the religion had taken over much of North Africa. Dating back to around the seventh century, slavery and slave trading existed in what was known as the "Arab slave trade" or "Islamic slave trade." But to refer to this slave trade as the "Arab slave trade" would be a misnomer as the Arabs were not the only ones involved in the Arab slave trade during ancient times. However, most of the rulers and raiders involved in the Arab slave trade process were Arabs, and most of the slave trade markets were located in Arab cities. But back in ancient times, the slave trades were named based upon the geographic location of the routes undertaken during the slave trades.

For example, the Arab slave trade was the intersection of slavery and trade surrounding the Arab world and Indian Ocean, mainly in Western and Central Asia, Northern and Eastern Africa, India, and Europe. Most of the slaves were captured mainly from Africa's interior, Southern and Eastern Europe, the Caucasus, and Central Asia.

You see, many societies in Africa with kings and hierarchical forms of government traditionally kept slaves, but these were mostly used for domestic purposes. They were an indication of power and wealth and not used for commercial gain. The slaves in Africa were given certain rights in a system similar to indentured servitude, similar to what existed elsewhere in the world. The slaves in Africa were seen as "people" and in most cases afforded limited or restricted rights and in some cases would be able to buy their freedom—meaning that the restrictions upon the slaves, for the most part, were temporary. The enslaved Africans and their descendants—those who were extricated from their homeland and dispersed throughout the world, particularly to the Americas—were treated as property, with no rights whatsoever, and the enslavement would be deemed permanent.

A "**HIERARCHY**" means:

* a system or organization in which people or groups are ranked one above the other according to status or authority.

It is important for you to know that Egypt, located in the northern part of Africa, was the first of many great African civilizations. It lasted thousands of years, and its people achieved many magnificent and incredible things—particularly in the fields of science, mathematics, medicine, technology, and the arts.

Morocco

Tunisia

Algeria

Libya

Egypt

Western
Sahara

Mauritania

Mali

Niger

The Sudan

Eritrea

Djibouti

Senegal

Chad

Burkina
Faso

Guinea

Nigeria

Ethiopia

The Ivory
Coast

South Sudan

The Central
African Republic

Cameroon

Somalia

Liberia

Ghana

Benin

Uganda

Kenya

Sierra Leone

Togo

Gabon

Guinea-Bissau

Equatorial
Guinea

Democratic
Republic
of the Congo

Rwanda
Burundi

The Gambia

Republic
of the Congo

Tanzania

Angola

Malawi

Zambia

Mozambique

Madagascar

Zimbabwe

Namibia

Botswana

Eswatini

South Africa

Lesotho

Most pyramids were huge. Inside, they had storerooms, bedrooms, and even inside courtyards. Pyramids took many years to build. The inside walls were also beautifully decorated.

Did You Know?

The most popular Egyptian achievement remains the pyramids. In ancient Egypt, pyramids were built during the time of the Old Kingdom. They were royal tombs where the ancient Egyptians buried their kings. The first pyramid was the Step Pyramid. It was built about five thousand years ago.

Did You Know?

The ancient Egyptians created the 365-day calendar based on the farming seasons. There were three seasons: the flooding season, the planting seasons, and the harvest season. Each season was three months long, adding up to 360 days. The ancient Egyptians noticed they needed a few more days to fit the seasons. They added five days, holy days, to thank the gods.

Ghana, located in the western part of Africa, once was a vast empire. It was once a highly advanced and prosperous place, particularly between the ninth and thirteenth centuries, when it traded in gold, salt, and copper.

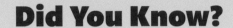

Did You Know?

- Africans were not the first, nor the only, people to be enslaved.

- Household slavery was an accepted practice in ancient Greece, as in other societies of the time. For example, it is estimated that during the fifth and sixth centuries BC, Athens had the largest population of slaves (as many as eighty thousand) with an average of three or four slaves per household, except in poor families.

- The Arab slave trade was in place for approximately 1300 years, having started around the seventh century BC. The violent transatlantic slave trade took place during the course of at least four centuries, having started around the 1500s.

- Under Islamic law, as it existed during the Arab slave trade, most slaves were treated as "people," with limited rights; whereas during the transatlantic slave trade, the enslaved Africans were treated as "chattel," or the personal possessions of others, and had no rights at all.

Chapter 5

The Transatlantic Slave Trade

*"So enormous, so dreadful, so irremediable did the
[slave] trade's wickedness appear, that my own mind
was completely made up for abolition. Let the conse-
quences be what they would; I from this time determined
that I would never rest until I had effected its abolition."*

—William Wilberforce

A s we all know, most American immigrants leave
their homelands in search of a better life. However, we African Americans are the only ethnic
group whose ancestors arrived in the United States
against our will via the transatlantic slave trade.

Whether arguably traded by enemy tribes or kidnapped
by European raiders, Africans were forced into what were
known to be slave camps, located on the west coast of Africa, starting in the 1500s. Slave camps were where many
Africans who were kidnapped from their villages were kept

under force to await one of the many slave ships that was used to transport the enslaved Africans to destinations throughout the world. If they managed to survive the disease and misery of the slave camps, they took their last steps on African soil at places like the Doorway of No Return on Goree Island in Senegal and Elmina in Ghana.

For centuries, slave traders engaged primarily in the trade of goods such as gold, silk, spices, and they secured slaves as "prisoners of war"; often those slaves were used for domestic and field labor, working on farms, in mines, and at mills. Europeans did not have power or access to the trade routes to India or China, which were controlled by the Muslims.

Having no way to access the trade routes to India and China, over land or by the Mediterranean Sea area, and in an effort to escape the calamities of poverty, disease, and the threat of the people of the Ottoman Empire (who were expanding their empire and seeking dominance and control over much of the territory located in a large section of Europe), sailors from Portugal, Spain, and other European explorers began leaving various parts of Europe with the hope of gaining access to Africa's gold, finding new lands, new trade routes, and new wealth for their respective nations.

Prior to the fifteenth century, European traders were primarily engaged in the trade of goods. However, in the fifteenth and sixteenth centuries, European merchants turned their attention to human trade after realizing how profitable the slave trade had become. Over time, slave trades became the most profitable source of providing free, coerced labor and thus contributing to the development, wealth, and power structure of many empires and monarchies.

In fact, between the fifteenth and late nineteenth centuries, there were four slave trades operating in a way that extricated, exploited, brutalized, and enslaved the Africans from every angle surrounding the continent of Africa. They were:

i.   the Arab trans-Saharan slave trade;

ii. the Arab slave trade to Asia;

iii. the Portuguese slave trade;

iv. and of course, the infamous transatlantic slave trade.

The Arab trans-Saharan slave trade engaged in the removal of Africans from the central, east, and southern parts of Africa. The Arab slave trade to Asia engaged in the removal of Africans from the eastern region of Africa, dispersing the Africans via routes along the Indian Ocean, throughout parts of Asia, the Middle East, and Europe, and via routes along the Indian Ocean. The Portuguese slave trade was responsible for the removal of Africans from the sub-Saharan part of Africa.

The transatlantic slave trade was the largest forced population migration in history, and since the mid-fifteenth century, it has created a coerced labor force for the sole purpose of exploiting the sweat equity of the Amerindians (Native Americans) located in the Americas. After the collapse of the Amerindian population, the attention was turned to the enslavement of Africans. Consequently, it would be the Africans who would dominate the ethnic group to be largely enslaved by Portugal and ultimately other European nations.

The transatlantic slave trade unleashed a war between nations, mainly involving France, Spain, Portugal, and England. Each nation believed that with the more land secured and settled and human trade engaged in, the end result would be that their respective nation would become the most powerful empire.

* * * * *

As for England in the late 1500s, Queen Elizabeth I had a financial and political interest in establishing colonies in the Americas. In an effort to expand the British Empire, she sent British settlers out on an expedition to sail across the Atlantic Ocean in hopes of landing on territories along the coast of the Americas. Her goal was to set up trade ports along the coast of the Americas.

In as early as 1584, Queen Elizabeth I sent British settlers to explore parts of North America, particularly areas along the coastline. The first group of settlers set upon an island off the coast of North Carolina, named Roanoke Island. However, over the twelve-month period that followed—with the settlers reaching the island of Roanoke, then returning to England to secure more supplies to journey back to Roanoke Island to develop the colony—the mission was unsuccessful.

In December 1606, after the first attempt by Queen Elizabeth I to establish colonies in North America failed, there began the journey of other British settlers who would voyage from England to the northeast coastline of North America to settle upon North America and establish British colonies for the queen.

In fact, she subsequently established several British colonies in the Americas, thirteen of which were established along the eastern coast of North America:

> Virginia (est. 1607), New Hampshire (est. 1623), New York (est. 1626), Massachusetts Bay (est. 1630), Maryland (est. 1633), Connecticut (est. 1636), Rhode Island (est. 1636), Delaware (est. 1638), North Carolina (est. 1663), South Carolina (est. 1663), New Jersey (est. 1664), Pennsylvania (est. 1681), and Georgia (est. 1732).

During the sixteenth century, Europeans who settled in the Americas were intrigued by the idea of owning their own land, and as such, they were reluctant to work for others.

During the seventeenth and eighteenth centuries, as European countries conquered many of the Caribbean Islands and much of North and South America and established colonies, the demand for free labor intensified.

The crops grown on the plantations in the new colonies, such as sugarcane, tobacco, and cotton, were labor intensive, and there were not enough settlers and indentured servants to cultivate all the new lands. (By the way, these indentured servants were people who immigrated to the Americas from other parts of Europe, like Ireland. Irish people made their way here though "indenture," which is another name for slavery.)

Even convicts from England were sent to work on the plantations, but there were never enough, so to satisfy the high demand for labor, planters (plantation owners) purchased more and more slaves.

Many of the Native Americans who occupied North America prior to the invasion by the Europeans were enslaved. Many of them died from diseases and in battles they found themselves engaged in with people from other countries; many more resisted, while others were subjected to a forced migration to other parts of North America. In fact, a large amount of the people who were enslaved over time (by the Europeans, initially) were darker-skinned Native Americans.

To meet the massive demand for new labor, the Europeans looked to Africa. Millions of Africans were captured, enslaved, and forced across the Atlantic to labor in plantations in the Caribbean and in America. They forced the enslaved people to work in mines and on tobacco plantations in South America and on sugar plantations in the West Indies. The enslaved Africans were transported huge distances across the Atlantic to work, with no chance of returning home.

The transatlantic slave trade is perhaps the best known of the many elaborate slave trade networks that developed over centuries. From the fifteenth century to the end of the nineteenth century, the transatlantic slave trade was responsible for the uprooting and forced migration of approximately twelve to fifteen million enslaved Africans across the Atlantic

Ocean. It was the powerful European peoples, such as the Portuguese, the British, the French, and the Dutch, along with the Spanish and other peoples, that played a major role in this forced migration of Africans across the Atlantic Ocean. This trafficking of millions of Africans was referred to as the *Maafa*—a term in Swahili that means the "great disaster." The trans-atlantic slave trade arguably resulted in the largest forced population migration in the world.

Several countries were involved in the forced migration of the Africans, and different countries were more powerful in the slave trade at different times. For example, from 1440–1640, Portugal controlled the slave trade almost completely. However, over time, the balance of power in Europe changed.

By the early eighteenth century, Britain had become the world's principal slave trading power. The British slave traders alone, via the use of thousands of slave ships, transported at least 3.5 million enslaved Africans to the Americas.

The British slave ships and merchants had such a domineering presence during the transatlantic slave trade that they not only carried enslaved Africans to the Caribbean, Brazil, and North America, but they also carried enslaved Africans to French and Spanish colonies, their main economic rivals.

Throughout the many years of the transatlantic slave trade, millions of enslaved Africans were dispersed throughout the Central, North, and South Americas, with at least two hundred thousand going to parts of Europe.

Chapter 6
The Middle Passage

*"I keep sailing on in this middle passage. I am sailing
into the wind and the dark. But I am doing my best to
keep my boat steady and my sails full."*

—Arthur Ashe

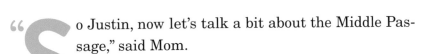

"So Justin, now let's talk a bit about the Middle Passage," said Mom.

"What is that?" asked Justin.

"Well," stated Mom. "You see, Justin, the transatlantic slave trade that we just spoke of is sometimes known as the triangular trade. It was referred to as that because it had three parts, much like three sides of a triangle. The Middle Passage got its name because it was the middle part of the triangular trade. The three parts of the Transatlantic Slave Trade were:

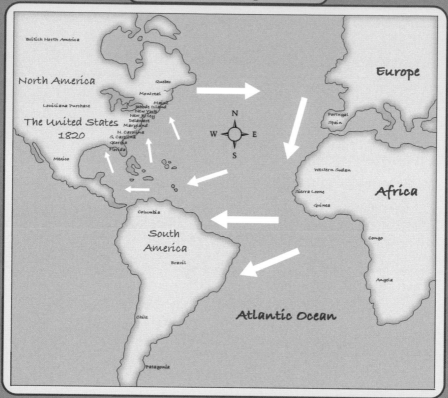

i. From Europe to Africa

"Ships brought weapons, gunpowder, cloth, rum, and manu-factured goods from Europe to Africa. In Africa, these mate-rials were traded for African people who had been kidnapped from their homes—snatched up as prisoners of war or in punishment of a crime.

ii. Africa to the Americas (the Middle Passage)

"Enslaved Africans were brought to the Americas on slave ships. They were sold as slaves or traded for raw materials like sugar, tobacco, and cotton that other enslaved people had made.

iii. The Americas to Europe

"The third part of the triangle was the return trip to Europe.

"These raw materials were sent to Europe, where they were used to make things. Then the triangular trade would start all over again. For example, cotton would be used to make cloth. That cloth could then be sent to Africa to trade for more slaves.

"Expanding on this process, the first phase of the transatlantic slave trade involved the slave traders from nations such as Portugal, Spain, England, France, the Netherlands, Denmark, other regions in Europe, and eventually from North America. They would leave their nations and sail along the west and southeast coasts of Africa, stopping at the slave ports in places such as Senegambia, Sierra Leone, the Windward Coast, the Gold Coast, the Bight of Benin, the Bight of Biafra, the Gulf of Guinea Islands, West Central Africa and Saint Helena, Southeast Africa, Indian Ocean Islands, and other African regions where the slave traders would engage in the trade of slaves for goods.

"During the forced migration, the slaves would be shackled and, in most cases, branded upon their bodies and then be forced upon the slave ships. They were then extricated from their homeland—the destination unknown to the African but predestined by the slave traders—to slave ports located across the Atlantic Ocean in the Americas (North America, South America, and Central America) and Europe.

"The second phase of the transatlantic slave trade process involved the enslaved Africans being transported via armed sailors across the Atlantic Ocean to the Americas. They were disembarked at ports located in the New World, at these places:

- **Mainland North America, in places like:**

  » Rhode Island, New Hampshire, Massachusetts, Connecticut, New York, New Jersey, Pennsylvania,

Maryland, Virginia, North Carolina, South Carolina, Georgia, Florida, the Gulf Coast, and other areas

- **Caribbean Islands (Central America), in places like:**

  » Hispaniola, Puerto Rico, Cuba, other Spanish Caribbean regions, Dutch Caribbean regions, Dutch Guianas, Tortola, Antigua, St. Kitts, Nevis, Montserrat, Dominica, St. Lucia, Barbados, St. Vincent, Grenada, Trinidad, Tobago, Jamaica, Bahamas, British Guiana, British Honduras, other British Caribbean regions, Martinique, Guadeloupe, French Guiana, Saint-Domingue, other French Caribbean regions, Danish West Indies, St. Barthélemy (Sweden), and other regions

- **Spanish mainland Americas and Brazil (South America), in places like:**

  » Spanish Circum-Caribbean, Rio de la Plata, and Peru

  » Amazonia, Bahia, Pernambuco, Southeast Brazil, and other regions in Brazil

Once disembarked in the Americas, the enslaved Africans were placed in the slave market and sold into slavery. The enslaved Africans would remain on the new land, having been sold to merchants who would exploit the enslaved African by making them domestic and plantation workers to toil the fields cultivating, harvesting, and preparing for export the newly-discovered agricultural resources. Some slaves, upon disembarking the slave ships, would escape into the mountains, forests, and lands in the "New World"—seeking refuge from the slave traders and holders—and eventually begin uprisings and rebellions.

The third phase of the transatlantic slave trade was the last phase where some of the enslaved Africans were made to journey what is called the Middle Passage—where the goods, products, materials, other resources, often labored slaves, and the newly-acquired enslaved Africans were exported to places like Portugal, Spain, France, England, the Netherlands, Denmark, and North America.

The enslaved people were packed onto the slave ships, often crammed together as closely as possible. Sometimes they were allowed to move around during the day, but many ships kept the people chained up for the entire trip. The armed slave traders would keep the women and children above deck, where they would be routinely assaulted, while the men were made to perform dances to keep them exercised and curtail rebellion.

Sailing through the Middle Passage could take anywhere from one to six months, depending on the weather. Over time, slave ships got better at making the trip more quickly. In the early sixteenth century, the average trip took a few months. By the nineteenth century, many slave ships crossed the Middle Passage in fewer than six weeks.

The enslaved Africans were treated terribly during the Middle Passage. They were not seen as human. They were thought of as cargo or goods—things to be bought and sold.

"Yeah, Mom," Justin responded. "That's what I was telling you about the rake in the yard. It's a farm tool to be sold or traded whenever the owner chooses. That's how the slaves were treated."

"That's a good point, Justin. It's also important to know that the slave trade was very profitable for slave traders."

By the eighteenth century, a male slave could be sold from about $600 to $1,500 (which is about $9,000 to $15,000 in United States currency today).

As a result of the money to be made from the practice of raiding the homes, kidnapping the Africans, forcibly removing them across the Atlantic Ocean, and selling them into slavery, it became more and more popular and profitable.

The slave trade finally came to an end due to a variety of factors, including the protests of millions of ordinary people in Europe and the United States. Its abolition was also brought about by millions of Africans who continually resisted enslavement and rebelled against slavery in order to be free. Resistance started in Africa, continued during the Middle Passage, and broke out again throughout the Americas. The most significant of all these acts of resistance and self-liberation was the revolution in the French colony of Saint-Domingue, now Haiti, in 1791. It remains the only successful slave revolution in history and led to the creation of the first modern Black republic. Haiti's constitution was the first to recognize the human rights of all its citizens.

First Denmark in 1803, Britain in 1807, and then other countries in Europe and the Americas abolished the transatlantic slave trade for a variety of reasons, including changes in their economic requirements. However, an illegal trade continued for many years, and slavery itself was not abolished in some countries until the 1880s. In Brazil, slavery continued to be legal until 1888.

Did You Know?

- When the United States Constitution was written in 1787, a generally overlooked and peculiar provision was included in Article I, the part of the document dealing with the duties of the legislative branch:

  » **Section 9.** "The migration or importation of such persons as any of the states now existing shall think proper to admit, shall not be prohibited by the Congress prior to the year one thousand eight hundred and eight, but a tax or duty may be imposed on such importation, not exceeding ten dollars for each person."

  In other words, the government could not ban the importation of slaves for twenty years after the adoption of the Constitution. And as the designated year 1808 approached, those opposed to slavery began making plans for legislation that would outlaw the transatlantic slave trade.

- A senator from Vermont first introduced a bill to ban the importation of slaves in late 1805, and President Thomas Jefferson recommended the same course of action in his annual address to Congress a year later in December 1806.

- The law was finally passed by both houses of Congress on March 2, 1807. However, given the restriction imposed by Article I, Section 9 of the Constitution, the law would only become effective on January 1, 1808.

- The new law had ten sections. The first section specifically outlawed the importation of slaves:

  » "Be it enacted by the Senate and House of Representatives of the United States of America in Congress assembled, that from and after the first day of January, one thousand eight hundred and eight, it shall not be lawful to import or bring into the United States or the territories thereof from any foreign kingdom, place, or country, any negro, mulatto, or person of colour, with intent to hold, sell, or dispose of such negro, mulatto, or person of colour, as a slave, or to be held to service or labour."

Did You Know?

- In 1803, Denmark abolished slavery.

- In 1804, Haiti became the first Black republic to create a constitution that abolished slavery and recognized the human rights of all citizens.

- In 1807, Britain and the other countries in Europe abolished the transatlantic slave trade for a variety of reasons, including changes in their economic needs.

- Meanwhile, back in Africa, while Britain had some success in stopping the slave trade along the African coast, the situation in the interior was different. There were Muslim slave traders from north of the Sahara and on the east coast of Africa who were still trading in land. Consequently, an illegal trade continued in Africa for many years, and slavery itself was not abolished in some countries until the 1880s.

- In Brazil, slavery continued to be legal until 1888.[12]

Did You Know?
USA—South Carolina

According to an article, "The End of the Trans-Atlantic Slave Trade," written by Nic Butler, PhD, a historian and staff writer for the Charleston County Public Library, "The federal law to close the trans-Atlantic slave trade on January 1, 1808, was enacted because the state of South Carolina—and South Carolina alone—was gorging itself on the African trade." He went on to say, "Our state and port city of Charleston in particular was struggling with an addiction to slavery, and the United States Congress intervened to cut off our supply."

In 1670, British settled and established a colony called Albemarle Point. "The first enslaved Africans came to South Carolina by way of Barbados, either at the end of 1670 or early 1671." Just six weeks earlier, the British ships "sailed into the Bridgetown Harbor in Barbados, where the colonists would pick up provisions and passengers. The colonists spent weeks learning the slave-based plantation system to be used as the blueprint for the economy that would allow the Carolina province to become a profitable slave-based plantation economy.[30] In 1680, the British moved the colony to Charles Town, now Charleston. South Carolina became one of the wealthiest early colonies largely due to the exploitation of slave labor, resulting in the export of cotton, rice, tobacco, and indigo dye. The South Carolina colony's economy was dependent upon the stolen labor of enslaved people that supported large land operations similar to plantations.[31]

According to Butler, "the total number of enslaved people brought into South Carolina was rather small during these early decades... The Royal African Company, chartered in 1660, held a monopoly on the English slave trade until 1689, and then a virtual monopoly until 1698, when Parliament passed a law that opened the business to any English merchant."[30]

According to Butler, "In 1699, the British slave trade increased significantly; and in the early 1700s, ships began arriving in South Carolina directly from the west coast of African, not just from places like Barbados, Jamaica, or Antigua."[30] He estimates, that "by the year 1708, it was clear that the planters of South Carolina, like their contemporaries in the West Indies and in South America, had become 'addicted' to the profits generated by the exploitation of their fellow humans."[30]

On April 5, 1740, as the result of the slave population growing so quickly, the South Carolina legislature ratified an act that was intended to curb the importation of Africans, imposing a prohibitively high tax on arriving Africans through 1745. This decreased the number of Africans who would be brought into the colony. However, "during the second half of 1749, the flow of African slaves into Charleston resumed like never before."[30]

Moreover, from 1750 through the 1760s, "the slave population grew so rapidly that once again, the legislature thought it necessary to intervene."[30] On August 25, 1764, the South Carolina General Assembly ratified another temporary law imposing a prohibitively high tax on newly imported Africans. "The tax had the desired effect because between November 1765 and February 1769, no new Africans legally arrived at the port of Charleston."[30]

> During the spring of 1769, the merchants involved in this trade set to work with unprecedented vigor. The rate of slave ship arrivals, and the raw numbers of Africans brought to Charleston in the early 1770s, far surpassed anything this port had ever witnessed. The clouds of war soon appeared on the horizon, however, and South Carolina's voracious appetite for fresh African captives was again threatened with disruption.[30]

For various reasons, between 1775 and 1783, the transatlantic slave trade was banned by all British and American colonies. The

American Revolutionary War ended in 1783 with the signing of the Paris Peace Treaty. "The end of war meant the end of the congressional ban on the transatlantic slave trade. By the late summer of 1783, South Carolina had resumed the practice of importing slaves; new slaves would arrive in Charleston Harbor. The import-export business was a major part of the economic fabric of South Carolina, but it took years to repair wartime damages and to negotiate the repayment of long-standing debts. Despite the return of peace in 1783, the American economy struggled to rebound after eight years of war."[30]

According to Butler: "March 28, 1787, the General Assembly of South Carolina ratified "an act to regulate the recovery and payment of debts; and prohibiting the importation of [Africans] for the time herein mentioned." He went on to state, "The ninth section of this law specifies that 'no [African] or other slaves shall be imported or brought into this state, either by land or water, within three years from immediately after the passing of this act.'" That is to say, no African slaves, newly-imported or American-born, were allowed to enter South Carolina from overseas or from neighboring states before March 28, 1790.[30]

> Less than two months after South Carolina passed a ban on importing African captives, delegates from each of the thirteen United States gathered in Philadelphia in the late spring of 1787 to debate the formation of a "more perfect union."[30] During that Constitutional Convention, which lasted from late May through mid-September, several delegates from northern states argued in favor of inserting language into the nation's charter to prohibit the growth of the institution of slavery. Ten states had already banned the importation of African captives. Men such as Luther Martin of Maryland argued that slavery was "inconsistent with the principles of the Revolution and had no place in modern America."[30]

In order to preserve the union of states, the delegates sought a compromise. South Carolina and their Southern neighbors accepted a proposal whereby Congress would not interfere with the transatlantic slave trade before the year 1808. Another compromise was to omit any direct references to slavery or slaves in the document so as not to offend those who found the institution repugnant. By September 1788, eleven state conventions (Constitutional Ratification Convention) had ratified the Constitution wherein Article I, Section 9 states in part:

> The migration or importation of such persons as any of the states now existing shall think proper to admit shall not be prohibited by the Congress prior to the year one thousand eight hundred and eight [January 1, 1808], but a tax or duty may be imposed on such importation, not exceeding ten dollars for each person.

On May 2, 1800, a federal act banned Americans from contributing to the growth of slavery in other places, but it was powerless to prevent the Carolinas and Georgia from exercising their constitutional right to import slaves for their own use.

At the close of the eighteenth century, not one state in our federal union was sanctioning the importation of African captives. However, in the early 1790s, the perfection of the cotton gin transformed cotton from a labor-intensive unprofitable crop into a very profitable international commodity. In 1798, with the acquisition by the United States of the Mississippi Territory (which included part of Alabama) and with the purchase, in 1803, of the Louisiana Territory, millions of acres of potential cotton fields were made available, inspiring thousands of agricultural men to head west and plant cotton. The new westward plantations would require labor, of course, but that commodity was in short supply.

After a sixteen-year hiatus, in December 17, 1803, the South Carolina legislature voted to resume immediately the importation of African captives.[30] "Starting in late December 1803, and continuing through the next four years, the Port of Charleston witnessed a mad scramble to import as many Africans as possible before government intervened again[30]… During the last episode in the long history of importing slaves into Charleston, the rate of arrivals into Charleston, the number of bodies packed into each ship, and the callous exploitation of the human cargo exceeded the horrors of all previous years."[30]

On March 2, 1807, US Congress ratified "an act prohibiting importation of slaves." This preemptive law simply stated that the importation of any person for the purposes of slavery shall become illegal on the first day of January 1808, and thereafter, it shall be illegal for any US citizen to participate, in any way, in the transportation of any people for the purposes of slavery.[30] On March 3, President Thomas Jefferson signed an act, a bill approved by Congress the day before, which states in part: "to prohibit the importation of slaves into any port or place within the jurisdiction of the United States." The act was to take effect on January 1, 1808.

On January 1, 1808, the act prohibiting the importation of slaves into any port or place within the United States went into effect. Notwithstanding the prohibition, the practice of importing slaves into any port or place within the jurisdiction of the United States did not end until 1860.

Chapter 7

The Resistance and the Resilience

"When your back is against the wall, there is only one thing to do, and that is turn around and fight."

—John Major

Since the invasion of Africa by the Europeans, the enslaved Africans have always put up resistance.

Did You Know?

- As the Africans were being kidnapped from their homes by and at the direction of European raiders, the Africans put up resistance, and many Africans were killed.

- As the kidnapped Africans were being marched from their homes to the slave camps and forts, located miles away, the Africans put up resistance, and many Africans were killed.

- As the enslaved Africans were being forced upon the slave ships bound for the Americas and other unknown destinations in Europe, the enslaved Africans put up resistance, and many of the enslaved Africans were killed.

- During the forced migration via the Middle Passage, there were:

  » enslaved Africans who, as a form of rebellion, refused to eat and died of malnutrition;

  » enslaved Africans who died of starvation due to the paltry rationing of what food they were given by the armed sailors, if fed at all;

  » enslaved Africans who jumped overboard the slave ships as a form of resistance and a sacrificial move to have their spirits freed;

  » enslaved Africans who died of diseases—diseases that developed under the inhumane conditions they were subjected to on the slave ships;

  » enslaved Africans who were murdered by the armed soldiers.

- Those enslaved Africans who survived the forced migration during the voyage of the Middle Passage were removed from the slave ship, branded, and taken to the market to be sold like chattel.

- Those enslaved Africans were then taken to the slave owner's home and forced to work, without pay, under the most inhumane conditions.

- Many who went to Central America and Brazil were forced to work in agriculture—planting, harvesting, and processing sugar on the plantations—often working ten months out of the year and sometimes working forty-eight straight hours around the clock.

Clearly, the enslaved Africans were never docile and passive people who simply accepted the brutal and inhumane treatment that came at the hands of the armed Europeans and from all others who engaged in the practice of dehumanizing people for the benefit of political and personal wealth and power.

Let's not forget that during the times they were being snatched up, kidnapped, and forcibly removed from their homeland during the transatlantic slave trade, or even while being marched across the sub-Saharan region in Africa, during the Arab slave trade, the enslaved Africans were under the control of armed foreigners—and the Africans had no idea as to the life they would be destined to live on the other side of the Atlantic Ocean.

The resistance continued on the journey during the Middle Passage. It poured into, and broke out, throughout the Americas.

Resistance to the institution of slavery was happening around different parts of the world, and it was happening as early as 869 AD. However, much of the resistance that started on the continent of Africa when the Africans were being snatched and forcibly removed from their homes and homeland and during the journey across the Atlantic Ocean poured over onto the North American British colonies and throughout other parts of the Americas.

According to an article written by Evan Andrews, "7 Famous Slave Revolts," several rebellions occurred throughout the world in which enslaved Africans rebelled against the Europeans and others who attempted to keep the slaves under their control.

The author of the article shows how several slave revolts broke out, particularly in different parts of North, South, and Central America. Here are six of the seven revolts noted by the author:

- **The Zanj Rebellion (869 AD):**
  - » Rebellion in the Middle East, long before African slaves were ever brought to North America.

- The Zanj (African) slaves went head-to-head with an empire. (Zanj is an Arabic term used to describe East Africans).

- The Zanj slaves joined Ali bin Muhammad (Arab revolutionary) and rose up against the Abbasid caliphate.

- With the promise of land and freedom, the Zanj slaves conducted night raids on nearby cities in order to seize supplies and liberate fellow slaves.

- What started as a humble revolt grew over time into a full-scale revolution that lasted fifteen years.

- **Gaspar Yanga's Rebellion (1570):**

  - Gaspar Yanga—an African slave—spent four decades establishing a free settlement in Mexico.

  - Gaspar Yanga is known as the "first liberator of the Americas."

  - In 1570, he staged a revolt at a sugarcane plantation near Veracruz.

  - Yanga, with a small group of slaves, fled into the forest and established their own colony, which they called San Lorenzo de los Negros.

  - They spent the next forty years hiding in this outlaw community, surviving mostly through farming and occasional raids on Spanish supply convoys.

  - Colonial authorities succeeded in destroying San Lorenzo de los Negros in 1609.

  - Unable to capture Yanga's followers, the colonial authorities settled for a peace treaty with the former slaves.

» Subsequently, Yanga, in his old age, negotiated the right to build his own free colony as long as it paid taxes to the Spanish Crown.

» In 1630, this municipality—the first official settlement of freed Africans in the Americas—was finally established and apparently still exists today under the name "Yanga."

- **The 1733 St. John Insurrection (1733):**

  » Slave revolt in the Americas on the Island of St. John in the Caribbean.

  » African slaves (mostly a part of the Akan—modern day Ghana) attempted to conquer the Danish-owned island of St. John.

  » Frustrated by droughts, widespread illness, and harsh slave codes, in November 1733, a group of the high-ranking Akans began to plot against their Danish masters.

  » Almost sixty years before the Haitian revolution, a group of enslaved Africans took control of the island of St. John and held it for six months against Danish and English forces.

  » In 1733, the population of the enslaved Africans on St. John was more than five times larger than that of the Europeans. There were 1,087 enslaved Africans and 208 Europeans on the island.

  » Slaves used smuggled weapons to kill several Danish soldiers inside a fort at a plantation called Coral Bay; most of St. John's command was seized.

  » In response, the colonial legislature passed the Slave Code of 1733 to try to enforce obedience.

» Penalties for disobedience were severe public punishment, including whipping, amputation of limbs, or death by hanging.

» Six months later, in May 1734, several hundred French troops arrived and violently put down the rebellion.

» Not until 1848 was slavery finally abolished in the Danish West Indies.

- **The Haitian Revolution (1791):**

  » The most successful slave rebellion in history.

  » Started as a slave revolt and ended with the creation of an independent state.

  » Inspired by the French Revolution, the Haitian (Black slaves) organized a rebellion, killing thousands of whites and burning sugar plantations en route to gaining control of the northern regions of Saint-Domingue.

  » The unrest continued until the French government officially abolished slavery in all its territories.

  » Toussaint L'ouverture joined forces with French Republicans and by 1801 had established himself as governor of the island.

  » In 1802, Napoleon Bonaparte's imperial forces captured Toussaint L'ouverture, and Napoleon Bonaparte's forces attempted to reinstate slavery; the former slaves took up arms once again.

  » Led by Jean-Jacques Dessalines in 1803, the Black slaves defeated French forces at the Battle of Vertières.

  » In 1804, the former declared their independence and established the island as the new Republic of Haiti.

» News of the first successful rebellion—the only slave uprising in history to end with the foundation of a new country—went on to inspire countless other revolts throughout the United States and the Caribbean.

- **Nat Turner's Rebellion (1831):**

    » The most famous slave revolts in American history.

    » In 1831, Nat Turner led an uprising in Southampton County, Virginia.

    » On August 21, 1831, Turner and accomplices killed his master's family as they lay sleeping.

    » Nat Turner and about seventy slaves went from house to house, killing over fifty whites with knives, clubs, and muskets.

    » The killings ended when the militia force intervened and Nat Turner and about fifty other slaves were captured and later executed by the state.

    » In the aftermath of Nat Turner's revolt, nearly two hundred slaves were killed by white mobs and militias.

    » This ensured repressive restrictions on slave populations.

    » Nat Turner's intelligence was seen as a major factor in his revolt; consequently, laws were passed making it illegal to teach Blacks to read or write.

    » In 1804, the former slaves established the island as the new Republic of Haiti.

    » News of the first successful rebellion—the only slave uprising in history to end with the foundation of a new country—went on to inspire countless other revolts throughout the United States and the Caribbean.

- **The Baptist War (1831):**
  - » Slave revolt on the island of Jamaica (in Central America).
  - » Jamaica's Baptist War ended with the death of over 600 slaves.
  - » Inspired by abolitionists' movements in England, on December 31, 1831, as many as 60,000 of Jamaica's 300,000 slaves went on a general strike.
  - » Strike led by a Baptist preacher named Samuel Sharpe. He worked as a bondsman; he vowed not to return to work until they were awarded basic freedoms and a living wage.
  - » Upon hearing that the British colonists planned to break the strike by force, the protest turned into an outright rebellion.
  - » This became the largest slave uprising in the history of the British West Indies. Plantations were burned and looted for several days, causing nearly $1.1 million in property damage.
  - » By the time the British army mobilized and put down the revolt, as many as three hundred slaves and approximately fourteen whites had been killed.
  - » Samuel Sharpe and three hundred additional slaves were later hanged for their involvement in the uprising.
  - » While it may have been unsuccessful, the effects of the Baptist War were felt all the way across the Atlantic.
  - » One year later, the British Parliament would once and for all abolish slavery in the British Empire.[13]

The acts of resistance noted above, which were happening during both the Arab slave trade and the transatlantic slave trade, each occurred as a direct challenge to the institution of slavery, which had been in existence for the past 1300 years.

As enslaved Africans were putting up resistance through uprisings and rebellions in protest to being enslaved, they not only shed their blood, sweat, and tears as their labor was being exploited here in America, but also made significant contributions in the military.

Almost immediately upon their arrival to North America, African Americans were enlisted to defend the British colonies whenever the colonists were under attack. However, at times of peace, the African Americans were excluded from military service. Nonetheless, African Americans are the only group who are known to have participated in every war fought by or within the United States, especially when fighting for America's independence. African Americans have participated in the following wars:

i. Revolutionary War (1775–1783)
ii. War of 1812 (1812–1815)
iii. Mexican-American War (1846–1848)
iv. American Civil War (1861–1865)
v. Spanish-American War (1898–1898)
vi. World War I (1914–1918)
vii. World War II (1939–1945)
viii. Korean War (1950–1953)
ix. Vietnam War (1955–1975)
x. Gulf War (1990–1991)
xi. War in Iraq (2003–2011)
xii. War in Afghanistan (2001–present)

Their service in the Revolutionary War resonates as the

most crucial war fought involving African Americans, as it was the war that helped to establish America's independence.

According to an article written by Patti Wigington, "African Americans in the Revolutionary War," African Americans made significant contributions to the Revolutionary War. The article points out the following:

a. "African Americans were involved on both sides of the Revolutionary War. Their contributions were made as both freedmen and slaves."

b. "Both free and enslaved Black people enlisted in local militias, serving alongside their white neighbors until 1775, when General George Washington took command of the Continental Army."

c. "Washington, himself an enslaver from Virginia, saw no need to continue the practice of enlisting Black Americans. Rather than keeping them in the ranks, he released an order in July 1775, saying, 'You are not to enlist any deserter from the ministerial [British] army, nor any stroller, negro, or vagabond, or person suspected of being an enemy to the liberty of America.'"

d. "Like many of his compatriots, including Thomas Jefferson, Washington did not see the fight for American independence as being relevant to the freedom of enslaved Black people."

e. "In November 1775, the governor of Virginia, John Murray, fourth earl of Dunmore, issued a proclamation—essentially emancipating any rebel-owned enslaved person who was willing to take up arms on behalf of the Crown."

f. "By the end of 1775, Washington changed his mind and decided to allow the enlistment of free men of color, although he stood firm on not permitting enslaved people into the army."

g. "Formalized discrimination against Black people who have served in the US military lasted from its creation during the Revolutionary War to the end of segregation by President Harry S. Truman's Executive Order 9981 in 1948."

h. "Although desegregation within the US military was legally established with President Truman's executive order, full integration of African American servicemen was not established until 1950 for the US Navy and US Air Force and not until 1953 for the US Army."[14]

As the British encountered the Native Americans, they engaged in trading goods with them and setting up farms, establishing permanency on Native American territory. Clearly, the French were not going to sit quietly and allow their archrival, England, to encroach upon and seize their (the French) territory. Consequently, the French began building forts on the land to protect their interests by keeping the British out. This caused much more tension between France and England, ensuring a rivalry between the French and the British. The rivalry led to the French and Indian War.

The issue during the French and Indian War was whether the upper Ohio River Valley region was a part of the British Empire, and therefore open for trade and settlement by Virginians and Pennsylvanians, or whether it was a part of the French Empire.

This war lasted for seven years, ending in 1763, with a victory by the British.

On February 10, 1763, the French and Indian War ended with the signing of the Treaty of Paris. As a result of its defeat, France was forced to cede the eastern part of the Louisiana Territory to Britain, and the western part of Louisiana was ceded to Spain as compensation for Spain losing Florida. (Although in 1800, France regained sovereignty of the western territory in Louisiana, due to financial obligations in Europe, Napoleon Bonaparte sold the territory to the United States in the Louisiana Purchase of 1803).

The British won the French and Indian War, resulting in new territories being brought under the control of England, but the conflict, which lasted seven years (1756–1763), resulted in new and unpopular taxes. Consequently, British Parliament again tried to raise revenue by imposes taxes upon the colonies. In 1773, the Tea Act was passed; unlike the two acts that would follow, this act was imposed to help bail out the East India Company (a company that was a major part of the British economy). In 1765, the Stamp Act was passed; this act imposed a tax on all paper documents in the colonies. In 1767, the Townsend Acts were passed, which imposed taxes on goods that were imported to the American colonies.

The imposition of these taxes infuriated the British (American) colonists. They felt that the taxes were an abuse of power by the British Parliament, and they refused to pay them. This was the catalyst that led to the American Revolutionary War. The war did not happen right away. However, there were protests and major events that occurred leading up to the start of the American Revolutionary War, namely the Boston Massacre and the Boston Tea Party.

Perhaps the most famous African American patriot was Crispus Attucks. On March 5, 1770, Crispus Attucks was leading a protest against taxes in the streets of Boston when he was shot and killed by British soldiers. The event became known as the Boston Massacre, helping fuel the outrage against British rule and spurring on the American Revolution. Crispus was the first man killed at the Boston Massacre, and his death is often considered the first casualty of the American Revolution. A total of five colonists were killed on this day.

Another crucial event that led to the American Revolutionary War was the Boston Tea Party. This was a political protest by a secret revolutionary organization founded by Samuel Adams (who helped to write the first written constitution of the United States, namely, the Articles of Confederation) and the Sons of Liberty.

In the 1760s, England was deep in debt after fighting the Indian Revolution for approximately seven years, so the British Parliament imposed a series of taxes on American colonists to help pay those debts (basically to gain revenue lost from the Indian Revolution). After this act by the British Parliament, Samuel Adams, who already had a healthy distrust for the British Parliament, and the European American colonists became fierce critics of England's authority in colonial America and viewed the British imposition of high taxes and tariffs as a tool of oppression. The European (American) colonists no longer wanted to be ruled by England—as they believed the British Parliament (England) no longer had the colonists' best interests in mind.

Key concepts and moments derived from the Boston Tea Party, which truly sum up its mission, were:

- "No taxation without representation!"—meaning the European colonists believed they should not be subjected to the imposition of taxes upon goods and especially tea by the British Parliament because there was no representation of the European (American) colonies in England.

- On December 16, 1773, a political protest organized by John Hancock (the first signer of the Declaration of Independence) and led by Samuel Adams and his Sons of Liberty was underway when, during the meeting, out of frustration in having to deal with the unfair treatment by the British Parliament, Adams stated, "No more can come from a meeting." Basically, he said, "Enough is enough; we must take action to protect our self-interests and liberation from England."

  » That evening, a large group of men (members of the Sons of Liberty) disguised themselves in Native American attire, broke up into small groups, and headed to the port city of Charleston, to the Charleston harbor. Some went to the Boston Harbor, boarded the docked ships carrying loads and loads of tea products, and began to dump nearly 350 chests of tea into the water.

Of course, this act of defiance by the European (American) colonists infuriated the British Parliament. Consequently, in 1774, the British Parliament retaliated by passing a series of British laws designed to punish the Massachusetts colonies for the Boston Tea Party—these laws were known as the Intolerable Acts (also known as the Coercive Acts and the Restraining Acts).

The Intolerable Acts consisted of five acts: (i) **the Boston Port Act,** which closed the Boston Harbor until all the tea was paid for; (ii) **the Massachusetts Government Act**, under which Governor Hutchinson was replaced by General Gage and Britain took control of the Massachusetts government; (iii) **the Administration of Justice Act**, under which British officials would be tried in England; (iv) **the Quartering Act**, under which colonists must quarter British soldiers; and (v) **the Quebec Act**, which established a new administration for the territory ceded to England after the French and Indian War. These acts placed harsher legislation on the colonies, especially in Massachusetts.

The American Revolutionary War

On April 19, 1775, the American Revolutionary War (also known as "the American Revolution") began. The Revolutionary War was fought between England and its thirteen North American colonies. The war ended on September 3, 1783.

When the American Revolutionary War began, it was estimated that three million was the population of the thirteen British American colonies, and approximately 600,000 were comprised of African descent. Whether it was as soldiers, patriots, or even spies, African Americans played a crucial role in the American Revolutionary War.

Early in the war, the Continental Army (formed by the Second Continental Congress after the outbreak of the American Revolutionary War—by the former British colonies) did not officially accept black soldiers. The British decided to take advantage of this and offered freedom to any black slaves or indentured servants who joined their army.

The Continental Army eventually started to accept free black soldiers in 1775. By 1776, slaves were accepted as well, usually with the promise of freedom when the war ended.

After many battles were fought, the colonies gained their freedom and the United States of America was formed in 1776.

The new government would be a democratic government with leaders elected by the people and balances of power to make sure that no one could become king.

The problem was this new government structure only served to benefit the white race in America. Moreover, built into the government structure was the racial caste system, where the white race was to be recognized as the superior group of people, and Blacks as inferior. A system of government whereby the government, laws, judicial system, educational system, housing system, land ownership, political system, and all the resources and privileges afforded people in America only applied to those of the European race, specifically "white" America.

After the war, most of the African American men who fought in the war did receive their freedom as promised. However, they soon found out that the "freedom and equality" they had fought for did not apply to African Americans.

The Peace Treaty of Paris 1783 was signed on September 3, 1783, which effectively ended the American Revolutionary War between England and the thirteen colonies that rebelled (colonies that became the United States of America).

Unfortunately for the enslaved Africans and America, slavery continued in the United States for over eighty years after the American Revolutionary War ended.

Despite their help during the war, the US Congress passed a law in 1792 preventing African Americans from joining the military.

Did You Know?

- According to the Constitution of the United States, which was ratified in 1787, "all men are created equal," but this principle did not ring true for the enslaved Africans. In fact, although the practice of enslaving Africans, particularly as chattel slaves, had been in place since the mid-1500s with the transatlantic slave trade, by the late eighteenth and early nineteenth centuries, it was not unusual for politicians, who would later become chief executives, to own slaves.

- In "How Many US Presidents Owned Enslaved People?" Evan Andrews speaks to the number of chief executives who possessed slaves during their lifetime, and some owned slaves while in office. Between 1789 and 1859, with eighteen US presidents in office during this period, at least a dozen of the chief executives personally owned slaves. Two-thirds of these chief executives owned slaves while in office. In fact, the construction of the White House began in 1792, and it was slave laborers whose blood, sweat, and physical labor helped build it.

- According to Andrews, "All of the earliest presidents (except for John Adams and his son Quincy Adams) owned enslaved people." He goes on to state:

  » George Washington kept some three hundred bondsmen at his Mount Vernon plantation.

  » Thomas Jefferson, despite once calling slavery an "assemblage of horrors," owned at least 175 enslaved workers at one time.

  » James Madison, James Monroe, and Andrew Jackson each kept several dozen enslaved workers, and Martin Van Buren owned one during his early career.

  » William Henry Harrison owned several inherited enslaved workers before becoming president in 1841.

  » John Tyler and James K. Polk were both enslavers during their stints in office.

  » Zachary Taylor, who served from 1849–1850, was the last chief executive to keep enslaved people while living in the White House. He owned some 150 enslaved workers on plantations in Kentucky, Mississippi, and Louisiana.

  » Andrew Johnson, who served as Lincoln's vice president before becoming president in 1865, had owned at least half a dozen enslaved people in his native Tennessee and even lobbied for Lincoln to exclude the state from the Emancipation Proclamation.

» The last president to personally own enslaved people was Ulysses S. Grant, who served two terms between 1869 and 1877. The former commanding general of the Union Army had kept a lone Black enslaved man named William Jones in the years before the Civil War but gave him his freedom in 1859. Grant would later sum up his evolving views on slavery in 1878, when he was quoted as saying that it was "a stain to the Union" that people had once been "bought and sold like cattle."[15]

Chapter 8
The African Diaspora

*"For to be free is not merely to cast off one's chains,
but to live in a way that respects and enhances
freedom of others."*

—Nelson Mandela

"While we move away from the transatlantic slave trade and the Middle Passage, let's shift our attention to a very important development that came out of the transatlantic slave trade. Let's talk about the African diaspora.

"Wait a minute—African di-a-what?" Justin interrupted.

"A diaspora. Well, it's pronounced di-as-po-ra; and it stands for the dispersion of any people from their original homeland."

"It is believed that tens of millions of Africans were dispersed throughout the world by the Arab slave trade. Additionally, it is estimated that twelve to fifteen million Africans from places like Central Africa, Ghana, Nigeria, and Cameroon (and other parts of Western Africa) were displaced by the transatlantic slave trade.

"In the context of this story, I'm talking about the dispersion of African people from their homeland of Africa who had been dispersed throughout North, South, and Central America.

"While Africa has a population of approximately 1.2 billion people today, it is believed that the African diaspora dispersed 140 million enslaved Africans throughout the world. This number represents the largest forced migration in history.

"It is believed that although the African diaspora is estimated to be about 140 million people, only 5 percent of enslaved Africans are believed to have been sent to North America, specifically the United States, while approximately 48 percent were dispersed to the Caribbean islands throughout Central America. Another approximately 42 percent went to Brazil in South America. In fact, the most populated countries in the African diaspora include America, Haiti, Columbia, the Dominican Republic, and Brazil.

"As a result of the practice of forcibly removing people from their homelands, today there are tens of millions of people of African origin who live in the Caribbean, the United States, Brazil, and other countries in the Western Hemisphere.

NEW ENGLAND GALAXY

January 24, 1773   Vol. 28

THE SLAVE SHIP *NEW BRITANNIA* IS DESTROYED!

THE MIDDLE PASSAGE - TOM FEELINGS

On January 24th 1773, the captive people aboard the *New Britannia* revolted. The ship, which was on the Gambian River in Senegambia, was blown up, killing everyone on board. This was one of the most dramatic forms of mass suicide witnessed during the Maafa/Atlantic Slavery.

"When the millions of people of the African diaspora were forcibly removed from their homelands, they took with them their languages, beliefs, craftsmanship, skills, music, dance, art, and other important elements of culture. As a result, today we're surrounded by the legacy of the slave trade in a multitude of forms. Some descendants of the African diaspora identify themselves as being African Americans, Afro-Latinos, Afro-Caribbeans, Afro-Brazilians, Afro-Costa Ricans, and even Afro-Cubans.

"Ironically, but not surprisingly, Africans in the diaspora share a common history and face many of the challenges in their countries as we face here in America as African Americans, meaning the enslaved Africans that were dispersed throughout the world were subjected to marginalization, oppressive conduct, and racial injustice and saddled with restrictions upon their lives that prohibited the enslaved African from securing land, wealth, and power, just as African Americans have become the most marginalized group in America today.

"As you grow older, you will likely witness some form of disconnect that exists between the descendants of the African diaspora, that is, African Americans not understanding Caribbean Americans, and vice-versa; Latin Americans not understanding African Americans, and vice versa; and some African Americans not understanding the African cultures, but it is important to remember that:

- Africa is home to many diverse countries and cultures, all with their very own unique history, inclusive of having many kingdoms, with kings and queens.
- Africa contributed to the development of astronomy, mathematics, medicine, architecture, and philosophy—and their studies of philosophy were practiced long before the rise of Greek philosophy.

- As a result of the African diaspora, the enslaved Africans were taken to different countries around the world, and when being dispersed, they were not only alienated from their homeland, but also from each other.

- Even while working on the plantations or doing domestic work in the landowner's home, the enslaved Africans were under strict supervision of armed white overseers who did not allow the slaves autonomy or any free time to socialize with others.

  » Notwithstanding these facts, always remember that as descendants of slaves in the African diaspora, we have much in common—starting with the fact that our ancestors very likely came from similar areas in Africa before being subjected to the forced migration across the Atlantic to North, Central, and South America.

- Our history does not begin with slavery."

Chapter 9
The American Civil War
(April 12, 1861–May 9, 1865)

*"Whenever I hear anyone arguing for slavery, I feel a
strong impulse to see it tried on him personally."*

—Abraham Lincoln

The 1808 law ending the importation of slaves did nothing to stop the buying and selling of slaves within the United States. And of course, the controversy over slavery would continue for decades and would not be finally resolved until the end of the American Civil War and the passage of the Thirteenth Amendment to the Constitution in 1865.

Just before the outbreak of the Civil War, there were numerous attempted insurgencies.

In 1859, on the plantation of former President James K. Polk (eleventh president of the United States) in Mississippi, his widow watched as armed slaves barricaded themselves in protest. In this same year, additional uprisings were reported in West Virginia, Virginia, Missouri, Kentucky, Illinois, and North Carolina.

In 1860, fourteen cities in north Texas faced arson from a plot between slaves and white coconspirators.

Leading up to the Civil War, the frustrations of the more than four million enslaved African Americans and those of the few freed continued to grow. By now, the following had occurred:

i. The enslaved Africans and the abolitionists were unsuccessful in petitioning the government to recognize African Americans as human beings and eradicate the practice of enslaving human beings.

ii. The Three-Fifths Compromise in the Constitution still permitted a state to, for the sole purpose of having political representation in the House of Representative, count an African American as only three-fifths of a human being. For all other purposes, African Americans were considered property to be owned by others.

iii. The Southern states remained in violation of that provision in the United States Constitution, Article 9, Section 1, which established amongst other things: *"migration or importation of such persons as any of the states now existing shall think proper to admit, shall not be prohibited by the Congress prior to the year 1808..."*

a. Not only had the Southern states not stopped the slave trade as required by law on January 1, 1808, but when the law stopped the importing of new slaves in 1808, the South continued to increase its overall political status and electoral votes by adding and breeding slaves illegally.

Leading up to the 1860s, there were growing tensions between the northern and southern states pertaining to:

i. States' rights (how much power the states should have versus how much power the federal government should have)

ii. The expansion of slavery into the recently acquired western territories (with each new state added to the country—it shifted the political power between the northern states and the southern states, thus creating a battleground between the North and the South)

iii. The institution of slavery

Did You Know?

Nearly five years prior to the start of the American Civil War, in 1856, the Supreme Court of the United States, the highest court in the land, rendered a gut-wrenching decision in the case of *Dred Scott v. Sanford*, wherein it ruled:

> Black men—whether free or enslaved—had "no rights which a white man was bound to respect" . . . moreover, the Court ruled that Southern slave owners could take their slaves—their "property"—to any part of the United States they wished.

According to an article written by Melvin I. Urofsky, "Dred Scott Decision," Judge Taney's gut-wrenching decision, at least to African Americans, was a major impetus to the American Civil War. The author of the article points out:

> On March 6, 1857, the United States Supreme Court ruled (7–2) that a slave (Dred Scott) who had resided in a free state and territory (where slavery was prohibited) was not thereby entitled to his freedom.

> i. African Americans were not and could never be citizens of the United States.

> ii. The Missouri Compromise (1820), which had declared free all territories west of Missouri and north of a latitude of thirty-six degrees and thirty feet, was unconstitutional.

The author goes on to state, "The decision added fuel to the sectional controversy and pushed the country closer to a civil war." He went on to write, "Among constitutional scholars, *Dred Scott v. Sandford* is widely considered the worst decision ever rendered by the Supreme Court. It has been cited in particular as the most egregious example in the court's history of wrongly imposing a judicial solution on a political problem." A later chief justice,

Charles Evans Hughes, famously characterized the decision as the court's great "self-inflicted wound."

At the time the decision was rendered in the Dred Scott case, 1857, the Supreme Court was stacked with justices who were in favor of the institution of slavery—five of the nine justices were from Southern states, and one other justice was staunchly pro-slavery.[16]

There were a growing number of abolitionists in the Northern states who thought slavery was wrong and evil, and they wanted slavery made illegal throughout the United States. But in the Southern states, the Southerners worried that as the United States expanded, they would gain less power. The Southerners wanted the states to have more power and be able to make their own laws. They feared that slavery in America, a practice which fueled their economy, was in danger of being eliminated.

This sentiment, along with the successful election of Abraham Lincoln in 1860, caused seven southern states to secede from the Union in 1860–61 to form the Confederate States of America: Louisiana, Mississippi, Texas, Georgia, Alabama, Florida, and South Carolina. In 1861, four additional states joined the Confederate States of America, namely Arkansas, Tennessee, North Carolina, and Virginia.

During the industrial revolution, which started in England in the late 1700s and lasted for more than one hundred years, the United States experienced tremendous growth, which resulted in a fundamental economic difference between the country's northern and southern regions. It was development of the textile industry, when items that were once made by people in their homes were now being made in large factories. Then came the development of transportation. These new developments changed the way products were made and how people worked and lived, especially in the Northern states. By the end of the 1800s, the United States had become the most industrialized nation in the world.

Though agriculture remained the dominant industry in the North—consisting of smaller farms that relied on free labor—the Northern states had invested their money into transportation systems, which included steamboats, roads, canals, and railroads. They also invested in the financial industry surrounding banking and insurance, and they invested in various forms of communication systems, such as newspapers, magazines, books, and telegraphs. The Northern states' economy was rapidly modernizing and diversifying.

On the other hand, the Southern economy was deeply rooted in large farms (plantations) that produced commercial crops like cotton and tobacco. The Southern economy relied on slaves as their primary labor force. During the industrial revolution, the Southern states continued investing their money in owning slaves. The Southerners benefited from owning more and more slaves as the price of cotton skyrocketed in the 1850s while the price of slaves grew commensurately. In fact, during the 1860s, three-fifths of the wealthiest people in the country were Southerners.

The Civil War lasted for four years and began on April 12, 1860. It was initiated in the early morning when rebels opened fire on Fort Sumter, located at the entrance to the Charleston, South Carolina, harbor. The Civil War ended on April 9, 1865. The Civil War was the deadliest war in American history. Over 630,000 soldiers died in the war, of which it is believed approximately 160,000 were African American soldiers.

After the Civil War ended, the infrastructure, particularly the transportation systems, was destroyed. The Confederacy collapsed. Slavery was abolished, and four million enslaved Africans were freed.

AMERICA DURING THE CIVIL WAR

Union states
Union territories not permitting slavery
Border Union states, permitting slavery
(West Virginia created in 1863)
Confederate states
Union territories that permitted slavery
(claimed by the Confederacy) at the start of the war,
but where slavery was outlawed by the U.S. in 1862.

Did You Know?

- On September 22, 1862, when President Abraham Lincoln issued the preliminary Emancipation Proclamation, it declared that as of January 1, 1863, all slaves in the states engaged in rebellion against the Union "shall be then, thenceforward, and forever freed."

  » However, the document applied only to the enslaved Africans in the Confederacy and not to those in the border states, who remained loyal to the Union.

- On December 8, 1863, Lincoln put forth his Ten Percent Plan, which allowed Confederate states to rejoin the Union provided that at least 10 percent of their voting population took an oath of loyalty to the Constitution and Union; under Lincoln's plan, any state that was readmitted must make slavery illegal as part of their state constitution.

- A faction of the Republican Party (known as the Radical Republicans) viewed this proposal as too lenient upon the Confederate states since they were the cause of the Civil War. The Republican Party was concerned that if there was nothing more put in place, African Americans would be subjected to slavery all over again.

  » The Radical Republicans put forth the Wade-Davis Plan, which required a majority (not just 10 percent) of voters in ex-Confederate states to sign the so-called "Ironclad Oath."

  » However, President Lincoln refused to sign it.

  » On April 9, 1865, Confederate General Robert E. Lee surrendered.

- Emancipation redefined the Civil War, turning it from a struggle to preserve the Union to one focused on ending slavery.

Chapter 10
The Reconstruction Era
(1865–1877)

"It was not, then, race and culture calling out of the South in 1876; it was property and privilege, shrieking to its own kind, and privilege and property heard and recognized the voice of its own."

—W. E. B. DuBois

Now that the American Civil War was over, having ended on May 9, 1865, with the Union having prevailed, it was time to rebuild across the country. Not only were hundreds of thousands of American killed on both sides—including the tens of thousands of freed and enslaved Africans who fought in the Civil War—but families were also affected, and the casualties were incurable for the next hundred years.

There were several relationship structures that needed to be revised, such as the relationship between the Union and the former Confederate states and the relationship between the recently released four million Africans and their former slave owners. I would add that there was one other relationship that needed to be addressed but was not—the relationship between America and the recently-freed four million enslaved Africans.

As to the former category—the need to rebuild the relationship between the Union and the former Confederate states—there was much contention surrounding this subject. People were torn as to whether the Southern states should be punished for causing the war by seceding from the Union; others thought that the Southern states should be forgiven so that the nation could begin healing.

I would submit that the latter category—the reconciliation between America and the 246 years of inhumane treatment the African Americans were subjected to at the hands of the European Americans—would never be directly addressed, not even four hundred years later! One can say that the closest America came to reconciliation with African Americans during that time was from the efforts of the US President Abraham Lincoln, who actually had the courage to sign into law on January 1863 the Emancipation Proclamation, which led to the abolishment of slavery.

It was clear to President Lincoln that now that the slaves were free, we must determine what must be done to help them integrate into the very society which kept them in bondage and servitude for 246 years.

By 1865, Southern states had repealed secession and accepted the Thirteenth Amendment—the abolition of slavery.

By March 3, 1865, the Freedmen's Bureau was created by President Lincoln and administered under the United States Army. It was designed to give support and assistance, including advising on labor contracts between freedmen and their former masters. It also was heavily involved in education, helping put in place programs to assist the former slaves to learn to read and write.

On April 14, 1865, about twenty-four days before the Civil War ended (May 9, 1865), President Lincoln was assassinated by a well-known, disgruntled Southern white male and his coconspirators, who hated the fact that the Confederates lost the war and that the Emancipation Proclamation was passed by President Lincoln, abolishing slavery. Upon Lincoln's assassination, Vice President, Andrew Johnson became president of the United States of America.

President Johnson, being a loyal Southerner, wanted a softer, more lenient plan put in place than what Lincoln had mapped out. All President Johnson required of the former Confederate states was that in order to rejoin the Union, they (the former Confederate states) agree to ratify the Thirteenth Amendment, which abolished slavery.

The Democrat Southerners agreed. However, ratifying the Thirteenth Amendment did not mean that the former Confederate states were in support of the move to abolish slavery—no, they saw this as an opportunity to increase their political power.

Prior to the Thirteenth Amendment, under the Three-Fifths Clause of the Constitution, Southern states were limited to counting only three-fifths of their slaves for the purpose of counting representation in Congress; however, post-ratification of the Thirteenth Amendment, the Southern states were now able to count all of their slaves for the purpose of representation in Congress.

This would ensure the return to Congress, the Southern Democrats, and in even greater numbers. The goal was to solicit the help of their Democratic supporters in the Northern states to help in the fight to prohibit the citizenship rights of the former slaves.

The Republicans in Congress were not having it. They created their own reconstruction plan. They basically required the former Confederate states to write new state constitutions that recognized the civil rights of African Americans before the former Confederate states could be readmitted to the Union. This would begin what is known in history as the Radical Reconstruction period. They passed four statutes during the Reconstruction Era, setting forth requirements and guidelines by which the former Confederate states were to be readmitted to the Union.

Nearly two years following the end of the Civil War, Congress finally forged a complete plan for reconstruction. Three measures were passed in 1867 as well as additional legislation the following year. The measures' main points:

- The First Reconstruction Act (a.k.a. the Military Reconstruction Act) was passed on March 2, 1867. It was passed over the veto of President Johnson.

  » Under this act, the Southern states were split into five military districts, and each was governed by a military governor (a Northern general).

  » It demanded that new state constitutions be written, which were required to provide for universal manhood suffrage (voting rights for all men) without regard to race.

  » It called for the ratification of the Fourteenth Amendment and the provisions of equal rights for each citizen.

  » It called for the enfranchisement of all citizens, except ex-Confederates, whereby all males, regardless of race, but excluding former Confederate leaders, were permitted to participate in the constitutional conventions that formed the new governments in each state.[17, 18, 19, 20]

- The Second Reconstruction Act was passed on March 23, 1867. It clarified who shall enforce the law set out under the First Reconstruction Act.

  - » In no uncertain terms, it clarified that the military commanders were responsible to register voters and hold elections in their territories.

  - » It amended the First Reconstruction Act, whereby, unlike before, it now required that every voter recite the registration oath, promising their support to the Constitution and their obedience to the law.

  - » It also altered the First Reconstruction Act with regard to the method of counting votes. In the First Reconstruction Act, the ratification of the Constitution required a majority of all registered voters.

  - » The Second Reconstruction Act changed this so that only the majority of votes cast were needed to get the Constitution ratified much more easily against the will of many ex-Confederates.[21, 22, 23, 24]

- The Third Reconstruction Act of 1867 was passed on July 19, 1867. It gave supreme power to the five Union generals overseeing reconstruction in the five districts of the South.

  - » Each district included several former states of the former Confederacy.

  - » These generals held the power to remove any official, elected or otherwise, from office if they believed the official to impede rather than expedite the process of Reconstruction.[25, 26, 27]

Notwithstanding the rigors of dealing with the Southern Democrats, on June 13, 1866, Congress managed to pass the Fourteenth Amendment to the United States Constitution, which afforded equal protection of laws to everyone, including extending the liberties and rights granted by the Bill of Rights to former slaves. The Fourteenth Amendment was ratified on July 9, 1868; it gave full citizenship to anyone born in the United States or freed slaves.

Moreover, on February 26, 1868, Congress passed the Fifteenth Amendment to the United States Constitution, which banned racial discrimination in voting. The Fifteenth Amendment was ratified on February 3, 1870.

However, "although ratified on February 3, 1870, the promise of the Fifteenth Amendment would not be fully realized for almost a century. Through the use of poll taxes, literacy tests, and other means, Southern states were able to effectively disenfranchise African Americans. It would take the passage of the Voting Rights Act of 1965 before the majority of African Americans in the South were registered to vote."

At the time, the lives of all newly freed slaves, as well as their political and economic rights, were being threatened. This threat led to the creation of the Enforcement Acts.

Did You Know?

- President Abraham Lincoln added Andrew Johnson, a Democrat from Tennessee, on the reelection ticket in 1864 (to run as vice president to Abraham Lincoln) only as a wartime bipartisanship gesture.

- Tennessee was never under military rule, as it had agreed to the terms of the Republican Northerners before the passing of the Reconstruction Acts of 1867.

- "Despite the implicit fact that the Reconstruction Acts of 1867 were intended to improve the situation in the South for Blacks trying to resettle after emancipation, it was widely resented by Southerners, who felt that the North was yet again attempting to impose their will on the former Confederacy."[30]

- President Andrew Johnson was referred to as the "Veto President" because with every attempt by Congress to pass the Reconstruction Acts, President Johnson moved to veto each one of them, but to no avail, for the Reconstruction Acts of 1867 were each passed by Congress.

- President Johnson was impeached by the House of Representatives for attempting to remove members of his cabinet who had supported Reconstruction, even as he vetoed it.

  » Johnson had violated the Tenure of Office Act, according to the House of Representatives, which had been enacted in March of 1867.

The end of Reconstruction was a staggered process. With the Compromise of 1877, military intervention in Southern politics ceased and Republican control collapsed in the last three state governments in the South.

This was followed by a period which white Southerners labeled Redemption. White-dominated state legislatures enacted Jim Crow laws and, beginning in 1890, disenfranchised most Blacks and many poor whites through a combination of constitutional amendments and election laws.

The 13th Amendment

Section 1. Neither slavery
nor involuntary servitude,
except as a punishment
for crime whereof the party
shall have been duly
convicted, shall exist within
the United States,
or any place subject
to their jurisdiction.

Section 2. Congress shall have
power to enforce this article
by appropriate legislation.

The 14th Amendment

...nor shall any state deprive any person of life, liberty, or property, without due process of law; nor deny to any person within its jurisdiction the equal protection of the laws.

The 15th Amendment

Section 1. The right of citizens
of the United States to vote
shall not be denied or abridged
by the United States or by any
State on account of race, color,
or previous condition
of servitude.

Section 2. The Congress shall
have the power to
enforce this article by
appropriate legislation.

Chapter 11

Black Code Laws

(1865)

*"You can tell the greatness of a man
by what makes him angry."*

—Abraham Lincoln

n the twenty-four days before the end of the American Civil War, President Abraham Lincoln was assassinated, and the country was forced to deal with President Andrew Johnson's ideologies, which stemmed from a former senator from Tennessee who was a fierce supporter of not only the enslavement of Africans, but who believed that the states and not the federal government should be left to decide what was best for its citizens' voting rights. Again, with the death of Abraham Lincoln, it was now President Johnson who must contend with the situation of the former slaves, mainly what their status was as freedmen.

The white people in the Southern states refused to accept the fact that the Emancipation Proclamation served to end the practice of people enslaving people. The Southerners were furious at the notion that, with the emancipation of nearly four million enslaved Africans, they could no longer exploit the free labor once provided by enslaved Africans.

From 1865 to 1866, the Southern lawmakers (an all-white governance), having been emboldened and empowered by the presidency of Andrew Johnson, passed laws called Black Codes. The main purpose of enacting the Black Codes was to set restrictions on the recently released four million enslaved Africans in 1865. The intention was to criminalize the actions of African Americans as much as possible and to force African Americans to replay the role of slavery—therefore restoring the rights of whites, especially white Southerners, to exploit African Americans as a labor force.

The Black Codes was an attempt, by the Southern legislatures, to grant certain rights to newly released African Americans. For example, African Americans, as a result of the Thirteenth Amendment, could no longer be enslaved; marriages between African Americans must be recognized under the law; and, depending on the state, African Americans could own land. However, they could not vote, they could not serve on juries, they could not testify in court in matters involving white people, they could not own guns like white people could, and most importantly, they had to go to work for white people. Additionally, African Americans were required to sign a one-year labor contract with a white employer; otherwise, white Southerners would call them homeless, and the African American would be subjected to arrest, beatings, and forced labor.

The Black Codes was basically an opportunity for the Southern state legislatures to use the power of the federal government to restart the planting system—in which enslaved Africans engaged in free labor—a system that collapsed with the adoption of the Emancipation Proclamation. The goal of

Southern legislatures was to set up a system of forced labor in which African Americans would be paid a minimum wage, thus effectively having no choice but to work for white employers—and doing so in servitude, again. It was also an opportunity for white Southerners to set up a system of restrictions upon the freed slaves, which would also serve to criminalize the conduct and movement of the freed slaves, causing them to be routinely imprisoned.

The Black Codes were passed within a government structure where the highest court of the land, the United States Supreme Court, the federal government, and state legislatures protected the supremist interests of white Americans—resulting in African Americans having no voice, limited rights, and no educational and wealth opportunities. Moreover, the Black Codes were enforced by southern white men, mostly former Confederate veterans of the Civil War and the white police forces of the time.

Fortunately, in 1866, the federal government passed the Civil Rights Act, which provides that all laws are to be applied equally to everyone, thereby abolishing the Black Codes enacted by Southern legislatures, which were codified to apply only to Black people.

Discrimination continued in America, but notwithstanding this, African Americans continued to create communities as freed people; they continued to establish independence and wealth with whatever limited laws, rights, and privileges they were afforded, particularly during the Reconstruction era. However, due to the resentment by Southern whites at the progressive prospects of the African Americans, this gave rise to propaganda about African Americans, forced segregation, lies, and lynching of African Americans—resulting in the rise of Jim Crow laws.

Did You Know?

The main purpose of enacting the Black Codes was to set restrictions on the recently released four million enslaved Africans in 1865. The intention was to criminalize the actions of African Americans as much as possible and to force African Americans to replay the role of slavery. Therefore, its purpose was to restore the rights of whites, especially white southerners, to exploit African Americans as a labor force.

In an article written by Nandra Kareem Nittle, "How the Black Codes Limited African Americans Progress after the Civil War," the author points out some pertinent facts about the Black Codes and its impact upon the lives of the African American after the Civil War, the effects of which continue to date—here are the salient points in the article:

- For the African Americans subjected to the Black Codes, "life after bondage didn't differ much from life during bondage..."

- The creation and enforcement of the Black Codes was by design, as slavery had been a multibillion dollar enterprise, and the former Confederate states sought a way to continue this system of subjugation.

- They may have lost the war, but they're not going to lose power civically and socially. So the Black Codes were an attempt to restrict and limit freedom.

- Losing the Civil War meant the South had little choice but to recognize the Reconstruction-era policies that abolished slavery. By using the law to deny African Americans the opportunities and privileges that white people enjoyed, however, the one-time Confederacy could keep these newly liberated Americans in virtual bondage.

Pointing out a loophole in the Thirteenth Amendment, the author goes on to state:

- The 1865 ratification of the Thirteenth Amendment prohibited slavery and servitude in all circumstances "except as a punishment for crime."

  » This loophole resulted in Southern states passing the black codes to criminalize activities that would make it easy to imprison African Americans and effectively force them into servitude once more.

- First enacted in 1865 in states such as South Carolina and Mississippi, the Black Codes varied slightly from place to place but were generally very similar.

  » They prohibited "loitering, vagrancy."

  » The idea was that if you're going to be free, you should be working. If you had three or four Black people standing around talking, they were actually vagrant and could be convicted of a crime and sent to jail.

- In addition to criminalizing joblessness for African Americans, the codes required them to sign annual labor contracts that ensured they received the lowest pay possible for their work.

  » The codes contained anti-enticement measures to prevent prospective employers from paying Black workers higher wages than their current employers paid them.

  » Failing to sign a labor contract could result in the offender being arrested, sentenced to unpaid labor, or fined.

- The Black Codes not only forced African Americans to work for free but essentially placed them under surveillance as well.

  » Their comings and goings, meetings, and church services were all monitored by the authorities and local officials. Black people needed passes and white sponsors to move from place to place or to leave town. Collectively, these regulations codified a permanent underclass status for African Americans.

- After the Black Codes swept the South in 1865, Congress passed the Civil Rights Act of 1866 to give African Americans more rights—to a degree. This legislation allowed Black people to rent or own property, enter contracts, and bring cases before courts (against fellow African Americans). Moreover, it allowed individuals who infringed upon their rights to be sued.

The Black Codes may have been repealed, but African Americans continued to face a series of regulations that reduced them to second-class citizens well into the twentieth century. It would take the activism of civil rights leaders, and the Civil Rights Act of 1964, to see this legislation overturned. [28]

Chapter 12
Jim Crow Laws
(1876–1965)

*"Our mistreatment was just not right,
and I was tired of it!"*

—Rosa Parks

O ut of the American Civil War came the Emancipation Proclamation with the ratification of the Thirteenth Amendment in 1865. Then came the Reconstruction era, which gave birth to the Fourteenth and Fifteenth Amendments. The Fourteenth Amendment, which granted citizenship and equal protection of the laws upon all people, no matter their race, color, or religion, was ratified in 1868; the Fifteenth Amendment, which was ratified in 1870, granted suffrage to African American men.

The passage of the Fourteenth and Fifteenth Amendments was an attempt by the federal government to enforce the rights of the former slaves in the South. However, by 1876, the Reconstruction era ended, and by 1890, the Southern state legislatures—Southern Democrats who did not support civil rights for African Americans—completely ruled the

'Jim Crow must go!'

Henry A Wallace

Jim Crow blights the lives of Negro and white Americans alike. For prejudice corrupts

Jim Crow Laws – To Kill A Mockingbird. TKAM.wikia.com.

South. This gave them a lot of power in the US Congress. For example, the then Southern Democrats were able to make sure that laws against lynching did not pass.

As noted in an article written by Nandra Kareem Nittle, "How the Black Codes Limited African American Progress after the Civil War," she quotes Connie Hassett-Walker, an assistant professor of justice studies and sociology at Norwich University in Vermont:

> "With the passage of the Fourteenth and Fifteenth Amendments, there was a shift over to Jim Crow laws, which were kind of a perpetuation of the Black Codes…you don't just flip the switch and all that structural discrimination and hatred just turns off. It kept going."

In 1896, the Supreme Court of the United States ruled in a case named *Plessy v. Ferguson* that these racial segregation laws (Jim Crow laws) were legal. They said that having things be "separate but equal" was fine. In the South, everything was separate. However, places like schools for African Americans and libraries for African Americans got much less money and were not as good as places for whites. Things were certainly separate, but not equal. Moreover, public education had essentially been segregated since its establishment in most of the South after the Civil War.

The legal principle of "separate but equal" racial segregation was extended to public facilities and transportation, including the coaches of interstate trains and buses. Facilities for African Americans, Native Americans, and other people of color living in the South at that time were consistently inferior and underfunded when compared to the facilities for white Americans. Sometimes there were no facilities for people of color.

In essence, Jim Crow laws mandated racial segregation for whites and Blacks in public schools, public places, and public transportation, as well as the segregation of restrooms, restaurants, drinking fountains, and private workplaces. Also, in 1913, President Woodrow Wilson, a Southern Democrat, initiated the segregation of federal workplaces. In essence, as a body of law, Jim Crow institutionalized economic, educational, and social disadvantages for African Americans and other people of color living in the South. The US military was already segregated. The rigid system of laws was designed to keep African Americans from experiencing any of their newly achieved rights under the Thirteenth, Fourteenth, and Fifteenth Amendments.

As noted in the article written by Nandra Kareem Nittle, "How the Black Codes Limited African Americans Progress after the Civil War," she points out:

"And Black Americans weren't 'separate but equal,' as the states enforcing Jim Crow laws claimed. Instead, their communities had fewer resources than white communities, and white supremacist groups like the Ku Klux Klan terrorized them."

She points out also that during this time, the "Ku Klux Klan begin to terrorize Black Americans…"

"You start to see the rise of lynching, and lynching was really about the message sent to the living people," Hassett-Walker writes in the article. "It might have been about punishing that individual person, but it was done to keep the other people in line, to say, 'See, this could happen to you.'

Despite the terrorist conduct of the Ku Klux Klan in engaging in mob violence against African Americans, particularly in those communities where African Americans were trying to make a life for themselves with the limited protections afforded to them through the enactment of the Reconstruction Amendments, African Americans embarked on a mission to secure voting rights and to build their own communities, businesses, educational opportunities, and churches.

African Americans continued to push back. They began to demand redress against the mob violence and lynching that was precipitated by African Americans attempting to vote, gather, and strategize through nonviolent protests the ongoing lies put out by white Americans. These lies, which stated that Black men were looking at white women or that they raped white women, were orchestrated by the white men who were still angry at the fact that over four million enslaved Africans had been freed almost five decades earlier.

The white supremacists fought back; by 1919, the Ku Klux Klan, which had been a sullen idiosyncrasy, became a national ideology. White supremacy and Jim Crow's power seemed invincible. The Ku Klux Klan made it their personal agenda to keep the newly freed African Americans separate from the white race and to keep the African Americans under the control of the dominant white race.

Over the next decade, the violence against African Americans became even more horrific. Dozens of race riots and confrontations broke out across America. This period was branded as "Red Summer" for the unrelenting racial bloodshed. This violence was demonstrative of how "Black Wall Street" led to the 1923 race riots as well as other pivotal moments in a time when African Americans had made economic gains but, due to the lies perpetuated by the white Americans, their properties were destroyed, their businesses were burned down, and they were run out of their own flourishing towns—towns where the dollar earned by the African American had made its way through the Black community and allowed some African Americans to develop home ownership, cultivate black-owned businesses, and secure quality education for their children.

Racial tensions escalated as African Americans, in an effort to escape the violence and injustice that plagued the South through the Jim Crow laws, began to migrate north for better opportunities. However, there were Jim Crow laws of the North that African Americans had to contend with as well. For example, the federal government, under the Fair Housing Act, established covenants placing restrictions based on race as to where African Americans could live and own homes. These restrictive covenants were intended to racially segregate Blacks from whites and to keep the African American, or any person who had one ounce of black blood in them, from securing housing or home ownership in white neighborhoods. The federal government was encouraging and demanding that their loans be protected by banks' enforcement of the restrictive covenants. This served to keep African Americans from living and owning homes in certain areas.

Nonetheless, African Americans continued to do battle with the powers that be. They began to use the power of the press and the power of the courts to help pursue their quest for freedom, equality, and the dismantling of discrimination and racism in America.

Strangely, in these most horrible moments of violence and bloodshed, seemingly almost daily, some of the bravest people in the world gave their blood, sweat, and tears again, fighting injustice, inequality, and for the freedom we all have enjoyed so far. One such fighter, Fannie Lou Hamer, stated, "I'm sick and tired of being sick and tired," and, "If I fall, I'll fall five feet four inches forward in the fight for freedom."

Here are some other notable people who were born and raised in the late nineteenth and early twentieth centuries, particularly during the Jim Crow era. These are people who have made a difference in the world by fighting for equality and justice, for African Americans, and ultimately, for us all:

IDA B. WELLS
(born: July 16, 1862)

Famous Quote:

"I am only a mouthpiece through which to tell the story of lynching and I have told it so often that I know it by heart. I do not embellish; it makes its own way."

MARY CHURCH TERRELL
(born: September 23, 1863)

Famous Quotes:

"Seeing their children touched and seared and wounded by race prejudice is one of the heaviest crosses which colored women have to bear."

"Stop using the word 'Negro.'"

W.E.B. DUBOIS

(born: February 23, 1868)

Famous Quote:

"To be a poor man is hard, but to be a poor race in a land of dollars is the very bottom of hardships."

JAMES WELDON JOHNSON

(born: June 17, 1871)

Famous Quote:

"I would like to be known as a person who is concerned about freedom and equality and justice and prosperity for all people."

MARY MCLEOD BETHUNE

(born: July 10, 1875)

Famous Quote:

"We have a powerful potential in our youth, and we must have the courage to change old ideas and practices so that we may direct their power toward good ends."

NANNIE HELEN BURROUGHS

(born: May 2, 1879)

Famous Quotes:

"High standards can be contagious. But it doesn't necessarily happen through osmosis. Sometimes you have to budge people into doing the right thing—either by example or in a more obvious way."

"A lot of people endured a lot of hardship, humiliation, suffering, and pain. The least I can do is be my best, live my best life, and treat myself and my surroundings with respect."

THURGOOD MARSHALL

(born: June 2, 1908)

Famous Quotes:

"Where you see wrong or inequality or injustice, speak out, because this is your country. This is your democracy. Make it. Protect it. Pass it on."

In fact, it would be in 1954 that Thurgood Marshall would argue and win the landmark case of *Brown v. Board of Education of Topeka, Kansas, et al. 349 US 294*. The Supreme Court of the United States, under Justice Earl Warren, held that segregation of state-sponsored public schools was unconstitutional. The court held that "such segregation in state-run schools was against the United States Constitution." The decision, known as *Brown v. Board of Education*, in some states took many years to implement this decision, even while the court continued to rule against the Jim Crow laws in other cases, such as *Heart of Atlanta Motel, Inc. v. United States* (1964). The other Jim Crow laws were abolished by the Civil Rights Act of 1964 and the Voting Rights Act of 1965.

Therefore, with the passage of the Civil Rights Act of 1964, discrimination based on race became a federal crime. If there was evidence of discrimination based on color, race, or national origin, projects involving federal funds could be discontinued.

One hundred years after the enactment of the Thirteenth Amendment (ratified in 1865), the Fourteenth Amendment (ratified in 1868), and the Fifteenth Amendment (ratified in 1870) and with the enactment of the Civil Rights Act of 1964 and the Voting Rights Act of 1965, their rights would finally be realized!

Did You Know?

As noted in the article written by Nandra Kareem Nittle, "How the Black Codes Limited African American Progress after the Civil War," she points out:

- During the one hundred years post-abolishment of slavery:

  » A Black American's act of "simply exercising one's right to vote could lead to a visit from the Ku Klux Klan."

  » "Employment options . . . for Black Americans remained limited."

  » "[Black Americans] largely worked as sharecroppers, which entailed working the land of others (typically white people) for a fraction of the worth of any crops grown."

» "To say that sharecropping paid poorly would be an understatement, and impoverished African Americans racked up debts in shops that charged them high interest rates on the supplies they needed as tenant farmers."

» "[Black Americans] who couldn't pay their debts risked incarceration or forced labor, much like they faced during the Black Codes."

» "The debt peonage system robbed them of income and locked them into servitude once again."

- Additionally, the police imprisoned Black Americans for minor offenses that were committed in equal numbers by whites, who were rarely arrested, if at all.

Chapter 13
Civil Rights Movement
(1954–1968)

---

*"One person speaking up makes more noise than
a thousand people who remain silent."*

—Thom Harnett, a civil rights attorney

C ivil rights are the basic rights that every citizen has under the laws of the government. In the United States, the civil rights of each individual citizen are protected by the Constitution. Civil rights for every person means that regardless of gender, skin color, religion, nationality, age, disability, or religion, a person should not be discriminated against. Civil rights include the right to free speech, privacy, religion, assembly, a fair trial, and freedom of thought.

The term civil rights comes from the Latin term *ius civis*, which means "rights of citizens." Anyone who is considered a citizen of a country should be treated equally under the law.

Throughout history, there have been different civil rights movements. Each movement fought for the rights of a given section of the population that was being discriminated against. For example, the civil rights movement in the United States was a decades-long struggle by African Americans to end legalized racial discrimination, disenfranchisement, and racial segregation in the United States.

Between 1955 and 1968, acts of nonviolent protest and civil disobedience produced crisis situations and productive dialogues between activists and government authorities. Federal, state, and local governments, businesses, and communities often had to respond immediately to these situations that highlighted the inequities faced by African Americans across the country.

The lynching of Chicago teenager Emmett Till in Mississippi and the outrage generated by seeing his abuse when his mother decided on an open-casket funeral mobilized the African American community nationwide. Forms of protest and/or civil disobedience included boycotts, such as the successful Montgomery bus boycott (1955–56) in Alabama; sit-ins, such as the Greensboro sit-ins (1960) in North Carolina and successful sit-ins in Tennessee; marches, like the 1963 Birmingham Children's Crusade and 1965 Selma to Montgomery marches in Alabama; and a wide range of other nonviolent activities.

The Civil Rights Act of 1964, enacted July 2, 1964, is a landmark civil rights and labor law in the United States that outlaws discrimination based on race, color, religion, sex, or national origin. It prohibits unequal application of voter registration requirements and racial segregation in schools, employment, and public accommodations.

During the Civil Rights Movement, there have been men and women who have led the fight for their own rights as well as those of others. In many cases, these leaders have put their lives in danger by standing up for what they believe to be right. Some of these leaders are shown on the following pages.

CIVIL RIGHTS MOVEMENT

IDA B. WELLS

Ida B. Wells

July 16, 1862 – March 25, 1931

IDA BELL WELLS-BARNETT was an African American investigative journalist, educator, civic leader, and civil rights advocate. She was born into slavery in Holly Springs, Mississippi (Mississippi being one of the eleven states that seceded from the Union during the American Civil War). Approximately five months after her birth, the Emancipation Proclamation freed Ida B. Wells and her family from slavery.

By the early 1890s, as a journalist, she gained a reputation as a clear voice against racial injustice; she became co-owner of the newspaper *Memphis Free Speech and Headlight*.

During her investigation into the murder of one of her friends, her research showed that the lynchings that were occurring frequently in the Southern states were deliberate and brutal tactics used to control or punish Black people who competed with whites. She arguably became the most famous Black woman in America during a life that was centered on combating prejudice and violence.

"Virtue knows no color line."

"I am only a mouthpiece through which to tell the story of lynching and I have told it so often that I know it by heart. I do not have to embellish; it makes its own way."

CIVIL RIGHTS MOVEMENT

MARY CHURCH TERRELL

Lorem ipsum dolor sit amet, consetetur sadipscing elitr, sed diam nonumy eirmod tempor invidunt ut labore et dolore magna aliquyam erat, sed diam voluptua. At vero eos et accusam et justo duo dolores et ea rebum. Stet clita kasd gubergren, no sea takimata sanctus est Lorem ipsum dolor sit amet. Lorem ipsum dolor sit amet, consetetur sadipscing elitr, sed diam nonumy eirmod tempor invidunt ut labore et dolore magna aliquyam erat, sed diam voluptua. At vero eos et accusam et justo duo dolores et ea rebum. Stet clita kasd gubergren, no sea takimata sanctus Lorem ipsum amet.

Lorem ipsum dolor sit amet, consetetur sadipscing elitr, sed diam nonumy eirmod tempor invidunt ut labore et dolore magna aliquyam erat, sed diam voluptua. At vero eos et accusam et justo duo dolores et ea rebum. Stet clita kasd gubergren, no sea takimata sanctus est Lorem ipsum dolor sit amet. Lorem ipsum dolor sit amet, consetetur sadipscing elitr, sed diam nonumy eirmod tempor invidunt ut labore et dolore magna aliquyam erat, sed diam voluptua. At vero eos et accusam et justo duo dolores et ea rebum. Stet clita kasd gubergren, no sea takimata sanctus est Lorem ipsum dolor sit amet.

Lorem ipsum amet, sadipscin diam no tempor labore e aliqu diam eos justo rebu gu takin Lorem amet. dolor consetetur elitr, sed diam eirmod tempor invidunt ut labore et dolore magna aliquyam erat, sed diam voluptua. At vero eos et accusam et justo duo dolores et ea rebum. Stet clita kasd gubergren, no sea takimata sanctus est Lorem ipsum dolor sit amet.

eirmod tempor invidunt ut labore et dolore magna aliquyam erat, sed diam voluptua. At vero eos et accusam et justo duo dolores et ea rebum. Stet clita kasd gubergren, no sea takimata sanctus est Lorem ipsum dolor sit amet.

dor sit etur sed irmod t ut gna sed ero et ea asd sea s est lor sit ipsum amet, sadipscing elitr, sed diam nonumy eirmod tempor invidunt ut labore et dolore magna aliquyam erat, sed diam voluptua. At vero eos et accusam et justo duo dolores et ea rebum. Stet clita kasd gubergren, no sea takimata sanctus est Lorem ipsum dolor sit amet.

Mary Church Terrell

September 23, 1863 – July 24, 1954

MARY CHURCH TERRELL was an African American activist. She was the first African American woman to earn a degree from Oberlin College in Ohio in 1884. Oberlin College was the first college in the United States to accept African Americans and female students. She began her career teaching modern languages at Wilberforce University, a historically Black college in Ohio. She spent two years teaching at Wilberforce College before moving to Washington, DC, in 1887 to teach at the M Street High School, where she taught in the Latin department.

During the late nineteenth and early twentieth centuries, Mary Church Terrell championed racial equality and women's suffrage. She did this even when her father, and then her husband, did not expect or want her to work. She became involved with the women's rights movement, focusing on the right to vote for women. She was excluded from women's suffrage by white women as well.

She saw how race and gender were hinderances to Black women, notwithstanding their abilities. In 1896, she cofounded the National Association of Colored Women.

"While most girls run away from home to marry, I ran away to teach…"

"I cannot help wondering sometimes what I might have become and might have done if I had lived in a country which had not circumscribed and handicapped me on account of my race, that had allowed me to reach any height I was able to attain."

CIVIL RIGHTS MOVEMENT

W. E. B. DU BOIS

W. E. B. DuBois

February 23, 1868 – August 27, 1963

WILLIAM EDWARD BURGHARDT DUBOIS was an American journalist, educator, and civil rights activist. He was born in Barrington, Massachusetts, a relatively integrated community where children went to school together, no matter their race.

In 1885, at the age of seventeen, he moved to Nashville, Tennessee, to attend Fisk University. It was while attending Fisk University that he saw how African Americans were treated, particularly by Southern whites. Here began his journey to stand up for the rights of African Americans.

In 1895, he became the first African American to graduate from Harvard University. After completing graduate work at the University of Berlin and Harvard, he became a professor of history, sociology, and economics at Atlanta University.

In 1909, DuBois became one of the founders of the National Association for the Advancement of Colored People (NAACP).

*"The problem of the twentieth century
is the problem of the color line."*

*"Education is that whole system of human training
within and without the school house walls, which
molds and develops men."*

*"The cost of liberty is less than
the price of repression."*

CIVIL RIGHTS MOVEMENT

MARCUS GARVEY

Lorem ipsum dolor sit amet, consetetur sadipscing elitr, sed diam nonumy eirmod tempor invidunt ut labore et dolore magna aliquyam erat, sed diam voluptua. At vero eos et accusam et justo duo dolores et ea rebum. Stet clita kasd gubergren, no sea takimata sanctus Lorem ipsum dolor sit amet. Lorem ipsum dolor sit amet, consetetur sadipscing elitr, sed diam nonumy eirmod tempor invidunt ut labore et dolore magna aliquyam erat, sed diam voluptua. At vero eos et accusam et justo duo dolores et ea rebum. Stet clita kasd gubergren, no sea takimata sanctus e Lorem ipsum dolor amet.

Lorem ipsum dolor sit amet, consetetur sadipscing elitr, sed diam non d tempor lab a d

Lorem ipsum dolor sit amet, consetetur sadipscing elitr, sed diam nonumy eirmod tempor invidunt ut labore et dolore magna liquyam erat, sed voluptua. At vero duo dolores et ea n. Stet clita kasd ergren, no sea ata sanctus est ipsum dolor sit Lorem ipsum r sit amet, tetur sadipscing ed diam nonumy tempor invidunt bore et dolore a aliquyam erat, am voluptua. At os et accusam et duo dolores et ea . Stet clita kasd gren, no sea nata sanctus est em ipsum dolor sit et.

Lorem ips amet, sadip dia t a dia eos justo duo c rebum. Stet clita gubergren, no takimata sanctus Lorem ipsum dolor s amet. Lorem ipsum dolor sit amet, consetetur sadipscing elitr, sed diam nonumy eirmod tempor invidunt ut labore et dolore magna aliquyam erat, sed diam voluptua. At vero eos et accusam et justo duo dolores et ea rebum. Stet clita kasd gubergren, no sea takimata sanctus est Lorem ipsum dolor sit amet.

orem ipsum dolor sit met, consetetur dipscing elitr, sed nonumy eirmod r invidunt ut dolore magna rat, sed vero m et et ea kasd sea sit m

et ei ut la magna aliquyam erat, sed diam voluptua. At vero eos et accusam et justo duo dolores et ea rebum. Stet clita kasd gubergren, no sea takimata sanctus est Lorem ipsum dolor sit amet.

et labore et dolore magna aliquyam erat, sed diam voluptua. At vero eos et accusam et justo duo dolores et ea rebum. Stet clita kasd gubergren, no sea takimata sanctus est Lorem ipsum dolor sit amet.

Marcus Garvey

August 17, 1887 – June 10, 1940

MARCUS MOSIAH GARVEY, JR. was a Jamaican-born political leader, publisher, journalist, entrepreneur, and gifted speaker. He was a monumental, internationally acclaimed Black philosopher who influenced the independence movement of every Black nation in the world, ranging from the Nation of Islam to the Rastafari movement (which proclaim Garvey as a prophet) and the Black Power movement of the 1960s. He spent his life working toward African self-awareness, self-reliance, and political and economic liberation. His ideas and beliefs became known as "Garveyism." Garveyism intended persons of African ancestry in the diaspora to "redeem" the continent of Africa and put an end to European colonialism. He started a "back to Africa" movement, hoping to give African Americans the chance to go back to their motherland of Africa.

"A people without the knowledge of their past history, origin, and culture is like a tree without roots."

"The pen is mightier than the sword, but the tongue is mightier than them both put together."

"If you haven't confidence in self, you are twice defeated in the race of life. With confidence, you have won even before you have started."

CIVIL RIGHTS MOVEMENT

JAMES FARMER, JR.

Lorem ipsum dolor sit amet, consetetur sadipscing elitr, sed diam nonumy eirmod tempor invidunt ut labore et dolore magna aliquyam erat, sed diam voluptua. At vero eos et accusam et justo duo dolores et ea rebum. Stet clita kasd gubergren, no sea takimata sanctus est Lorem ipsum dolor sit amet. Lorem ipsum dolor sit amet, consetetur sadipscing elitr, sed diam nonumy eirmod tempor invidunt ut labore et dolore magna aliquyam erat, sed diam voluptua. At vero eos et accusam et justo duo dolores et ea rebum. Stet clita kasd gubergren, no sea takimata sanctus est Lorem ipsum dolor sit amet.

Lorem ipsum dolor sit amet, consetetur sadipscing elitr, sed diam nonumy eirmod tempor invidunt ut labore et dolore magna aliquyam erat, sed diam voluptua. At vero eos et accusam et justo duo dolores et ea rebum. Stet clita kasd gubergren, no sea takimata sanctus est Lorem ipsum dolor sit amet. Lorem ipsum dolor sit amet, consetetur sadipscing elitr, sed diam nonumy eirmod tempor invidunt ut labore et dolore magna aliquyam erat, sed diam voluptua. At vero eos et accusam et justo duo dolores et ea rebum. Stet clita kasd gubergren, no sea takimata sanctus est Lorem ipsum dolor sit amet.

Lorem ipsum dolor sit amet, consetetur sadipscing elitr, sed diam nonumy eirmod tempor invidunt ut labore et dolore magna aliquyam erat, sed diam voluptua. At vero eos et accusam et justo duo dolores et ea rebum. Stet clita kasd gubergren, no sea takimata sanctus est Lorem ipsum dolor sit amet. Lorem ipsum dolor sit amet, consetetur sadipscing elitr, sed diam nonumy eirmod tempor invidunt ut labore et dolore magna aliquyam erat, sed diam voluptua. At vero eos et accusam et justo duo dolores et ea rebum. Stet clita kasd gubergren, no sea takimata sanctus est Lorem ipsum dolor sit amet.

James Farmer, Jr.

January 12, 1920 – July 9, 1999

JAMES LEONARD FARMER, JR. was a civil rights activist and leader in the Civil Rights Movement. He was a child prodigy. His father was a professor at Wiley College and a prominent figure and influence in James Farmer's life.

At the age of fourteen, James Farmer, Jr. enrolled at Wiley College (an HBCU in Marshall Texas). While at Wiley College, he joined the debate team. He debated in front of nearly two thousand people during the debate against the University of South Carolina (the reigning champions), and it was Farmer's phrase "Stop lynchings now!" that garnered him a standing ovation.

In 1941, Farmer, Jr. graduated from Howard University.

In 1942, Farmer, Jr. cofounded the Congress of Racial Equality (formerly known as the Committee of Racial Equality). He was dedicated to ending segregation in the United States. He employed the tactics of nonviolence to further this cause. He was instrumental in organizing the sit-ins that were common, particularly in the Southern states. Farmer, Jr. was the initiator and organizer of the first Freedom Ride in 1961, which eventually led to the desegregation of interstate transportation in the United States.

"Courage, after all, is not being unafraid, but doing what needs to be done in spite of fear."

"Institutional practices, it seems, perpetuate themselves mostly by their invisibility."

"We do what we have to, so we can do what we want to."

CIVIL RIGHTS MOVEMENT

FANNIE LOU HAMER

Lorem ipsum dolor sit amet, consetetur sadipscing elitr, sed diam nonumy eirmod tempor invidunt ut labore et dolore magna aliquyam erat, sed diam voluptua. At vero eos et accusam et justo duo dolores et rebum. Stet clita kasd gubergren, no sea takimata sanctus Lorem ipsum dolor amet. Lorem dolor sit consetetur sa elitr, sed diam eirmod tempor ut labore et magna aliquyam sed diam volu vero eos et ac justo duo dolor rebum. Stet cli gubergren, no takimata sanctus Lorem ipsum dolor amet.

Lorem ipsum dolor sit amet, consetetur sadipscing elitr, sed diam

Lorem ipsum dolor sit amet, consetetur sadipscing elitr, sed diam nonumy eirmod tempor invidunt ut dolore et dolore magna aliquyam erat, sed voluptua. At vero et accusam et duo dolores et ea Stet clita kasd gren, no sea sum dolor sit Lorem ipsum sit amet, tur sadipscing diam nonumy tempor invidunt ore et dolore aliquyam erat, am voluptua. At eos et accusam et duo dolores et ea m. Stet clita kasd bergren, no sea kimata sanctus est orem ipsum dolor sit amet.

Lorem ipsum amet, co sadipscing diam no tempor labore aliqu diam eos just reb gu ta Lo am doi cons elitr, eirmod ut labo magna a sed diam vero eos et accusam justo duo dolores et ea rebum. Stet clita kasd gubergren, no sea takimata sanctus est Lorem ipsum dolor sit amet.

duo dolores et ea rebum. Stet clita kasd gubergren, no sea takimata sanctus est Lorem ipsum dolor sit amet.

rem ipsum dolor sit nt, consetetur cing elitr, sed numy eirmod nvidunt ut lore magna erat, sed At vero usam et es et ea a kasd o sea est sit um voluptua. At vero eos et accusam et justo duo dolores et ea rebum. Stet clita kasd gubergren, no sea takimata sanctus est Lorem ipsum dolor sit amet.

Fannie Lou Hamer

October 6, 1917 – March 14, 1977

FANNIE LOU HAMER was an African American voting and women's rights activist, community organizer, and a leader in the Civil Rights Movement. She was born in Montgomery County, Mississippi. She grew up in poverty. At twenty-seven years old, she married Perry Hamer, and they both worked on the Mississippi plantation owned by B. D. Marlowe.

In the summer of 1961, Hamer attended a meeting led by volunteers of the Student Nonviolent Coordinating Committee (SNCC) and the Southern Christian Leadership Conference (SCLC). She learned of the constitutional right to vote and the efforts of others to deny such a right to African Americans. She became a member of SNCC and in 1962 led seventeen volunteers to register to vote at the Indianola, Mississippi Courthouse. There, she was denied the right to vote due to an unfair literacy test.

After attending a program that teaches one how to pass the literacy test, she and a few others headed to the courthouse to register to vote. When the bus was approximately twenty-five miles of the voter registration headquarters, the bus driver stopped at a restaurant, allowing folks to get some food and to use the restrooms. That effort was immediately thwarted. For no comprehensible reason, Fannie Hamer and others were arrested. The bus driver was fined one hundred dollars for charges that the bus was too yellow—it looked too much like a school bus, was the allegation. Ms. Hamer was taken to jail along with several others, where she was brutally beaten at the direction of and at the hands of the police at the jailhouse. She sustained lifelong injuries: a blood clot in the artery in her left eye, permanent injury to her right kidney, and a severe leg injury.

The brutal beatings were some of the things African Americans went through, particularly in the Southern states like Mississippi, when all they attempted to do was exercise their right to vote, while simultaneously requesting to be treated like human beings.

The Justice Department brought a lawsuit against the five law officials involved in the false arrest and brutalization of Ms. Hamer and the other four people who were arrested with her.

The Justice Department brought forward the waitresses in the restaurant, the bus driver, and the two black men the prison officers forced to beat Ms. Hamer with the blackjack, before the officers further beat Ms. Hamer in her head with the blackjack themselves. Each of them told the court that Ms. Hamer and the other four people from the bus did not do anything wrong the day they were arrested. However, the officers were not found to have violated anyone's civil rights.

After three attempts at taking the literacy test, Ms. Hamer was successful and became a registered voter in the state of Mississippi.

In 1964, Ms. Hamer helped cofound the Mississippi Freedom Democratic Party. In August of that year, she attended the Democratic National Convention in Atlantic City, New Jersey, where she challenged the seating of the regular delegation from Mississippi. They offered Ms. Hamer two votes at-large as a compromise in the convention, but she did not accept the compromise, stating that after one hundred years of having the legal right to vote with the passing of the Fifteenth Amendment in 1865 and with having more than sixty-three thousand registered with the Mississippi Freedom Democratic Party, two votes at-large did not mean anything.

In January 1965, Ms. Hamer and two other candidates from the Freedom Democratic Party went to the door of the House of Representatives (knowing they would not be permitted to enter) to contest the seating of the five representatives of Mississippi, and they were turned away without being able to even go in to contest their seating. Their concerns were primarily to explain that in a state where 42 percent of the population couldn't register, these five representatives were not representing all the people of the state of Mississippi. Ms. Hamer and the other two candidates were ready to state that it was time that someone be in Congress who truly represented the people of the state of Mississippi.

Apparently, on that date, 149 Congressmen stood up against these five people looking to be seated. Ms. Hamer saw this as some progress. She remained committed to the cause.

In 1971, Ms. Hamer ran for the Mississippi State Senate.

Note: Ms. Hamer was not interested in the voting bill that was passed a week prior in 1965. She pointed out, "I am not looking for a voting rights bill in 1965 when in 1870, with the passage of the Fifteenth Amendment, we were afforded the same voting rights then as they are offering us now in 1965." As she correctly pointed out, with the passage of the Fifteenth Amendment and as part of the agreement to allow Mississippi, a former Confederate state, to reenter the Union, the state of Mississippi must agree to not do anything to disenfranchise the African American voting rights. She rightfully pointed out that there was a violation of the Thirteenth, Fourteenth, and Fifteenth Amendments to the Constitution that should be addressed.

"Forget what hurt you, but never forget what it taught you."

"If I fall, I'll fall five feet four inches forward in the fight for freedom."

"Never to forget where you came from, and always praise the bridges that carried us over."

CIVIL RIGHTS MOVEMENT

MARTIN LUTHER KING, JR.

Lorem ipsum dolor sit amet, consetetur sadipscing elitr, sed diam nonumy eirmod tempor invidunt labore et dolore m aliquyam erat diam voluptua. A eos et accusa justo duo dolores rebum. Stet clit gubergren, takimata sanc Lorem ipsum d amet. Lorem dolor sit a consetetur sadi elitr, sed diam n eirmod tempor inv ut labore et d magna aliquyam sed diam voluptu vero eos et accusa justo duo dolores rebum. Stet clita k gubergren, takimata sanctus Lorem ipsum dolor amet.

dolor sit etur ed d

Lorem ipsum dolor sit amet, consetetur sadipscing elitr, sed diam nonumy eirmod tempor invidunt ut labore et dolore magna aliquyam erat, sed diam voluptua. At vero eos et accusam et justo duo dolores et ea rebum. Stet clita kasd gubergren, no sea takimata sanctus est orem ipsum dolor sit et. Lorem ipsum lor sit amet, nsetetur sadipscing sed diam nonumy mod tempor invidunt labore et dolore gna aliquyam erat, d diam voluptua. At vero eos et accusam et justo duo dolores et ea rebum. Stet clita kasd gubergren, no sea kimata sanctus est rem ipsum dolor sit et.

Lorem ipsum dolo amet, con sadipscin diam te labor aliqu diam eos justo du rebum. S gubergr takimata Lorem ipsum amet. Lore dolor sit consetetur sadi elitr, sed diam n eirmod tempor invid ut labore et dolo magna aliquyam erat sed diam voluptua. At vero eos et accusam et justo duo dolores et ea rebum. Stet clita kasd gubergren, no sea takimata sanctus est Lorem ipsum dolor sit amet.

dolor sit nsetetur elitr, sed y eirmod dunt ut e magna rat, sed At vero usam et res et ea clita kasd no sea anctus est m dolor sit orem ipsum sit amet, etur sadipscing ed diam nonumy d tempor invidunt labore et dolore nagna aliquyam erat, sed diam voluptua. At vero eos et accusam et justo duo dolores et ea rebum. Stet clita kasd gubergren, no sea takimata sanctus est Lorem ipsum dolor sit amet.

Lorem ipsum dolor sit amet, consetetur sadipscing elitr, sed diam nonumy eirmod tempor invidunt ut labore et dolore magna aliquyam erat, sed diam voluptua. At vero eos et accusam et justo duo dolores et ea rebum. Stet clita kasd gubergren, no sea takimata sanctus est Lorem ipsum dolor sit amet.

Dr. Martin Luther King, Jr.

January 15, 1929 – April 4, 1968

THE REVEREND DR. MARTIN LUTHER KING, JR.
became the most visible spokesperson and leader in the Civil Rights Movement from 1954 until his death in 1968. Born in Atlanta, King is best known for advancing civil rights through nonviolence and civil disobedience, tactics his Christian beliefs and the nonviolent activism of Mahatma Gandhi helped inspire. Martin Luther King, Jr. stood for faith, equality, and nonviolence throughout his life.

In 1955, Dr. King led the Montgomery Bus Boycott.

In 1963, Dr. King helped organize the March on Washington, where he delivered his famous "I Have a Dream" speech.

In 1964, Dr. King won the Nobel Peace Prize for combating racial inequality through nonviolent resistance.

In 1968, Dr. King was planning a national occupation of Washington, DC, to be called the Poor People's Campaign, when he was assassinated on April 4 in Memphis, Tennessee.

"Our lives begin to end the day we become silent about things that matter."

"Injustice anywhere is a threat to justice everywhere."

"The ultimate measure of a man is not where he stands in moments of comfort and convenience but where he stands at times of challenge and controversy."

CIVIL RIGHTS MOVEMENT

BARBARA JORDAN

Lorem ipsum dolor sit amet, consetetur sadipscing elitr, sed diam nonumy eirmod tempor invidunt ut labore et dolore magna aliquyam erat, sed diam voluptua. At vero eos et accusam et justo duo dolores et rebum. Stet clita kasd gubergren, no sea takimata sanctus Lorem ipsum dolor amet. Lorem i dolor sit a consetetur sadi elitr, sed diam n eirmod tempor in ut labore et de magna aliquyam sed diam voluptua vero eos et accusam justo duo dolores e rebum. Stet clita kas gubergren, no sea takimata sanctus e Lorem ipsum dolor si amet.

Lorem ipsum dolor sit amet, consetetur sadipscing elitr, sed diam nonumy eirmod nt ut na d vero eos et accusam e justo duo dolores et ea rebum. Stet clita kasd ubergren, no sea kimata sanctus est em ipsum dolor sit et. Lorem ipsum lor sit amet, nsetetur sadipscing , sed diam nonumy od tempor invidunt abore et dolore gna aliquyam erat, diam voluptua. At ero eos et accusam et usto duo dolores et ea ebum. Stet clita kasd ubergren, no sea takimata sanctus est Lorem ipsum dolor sit amet.

Lorem ipsum dolor sit amet, consetetur sadipscing elitr, sed diam nonumy eirmod tempor invidunt ut labore et dolore magna aliquyam erat, sed diam voluptua. At vero eos et accusam et justo duo dolores et ea rebum. Stet clita kasd gubergren, no sea takimata sanctus est Lorem ipsum dolor sit amet. Lorem ipsum dolor sit amet, consetetur sadipscing elitr, sed diam nonumy eirmod tempor invidunt ut labore et dolore magna aliquyam erat, sed diam voluptua. At vero eos et accusam et justo duo dolores et ea rebum. Stet clita kasd gubergren, no sea takimata sanctus est Lorem ipsum dolor sit amet.

Lorem ipsum dolor sit amet, consetetur sadipscing elitr, sed diam nonumy eirmod tempor invidunt labore et dolo aliquyam diam volu eos et justo duo d rebum. Stet c gubergren, takimata sanc Lorem ipsum d amet. Lorem dolor sit consetetur sadi elitr, sed diam no eirmod tempor invidun ut labore et dolore magna aliquyam erat, sed diam voluptua. At vero eos et accusam et justo duo dolores et ea rebum. Stet clita kasd gubergren, no sea takimata sanctus est Lorem ipsum dolor sit amet.

Lorem ipsum dolor sit amet, consetetur sadipscing elitr, sed diam nonumy eirmod tempor invidunt ut labore et dolore magna erat, sed a. At vero cusam et olores et ea et clita kasd en, no sea sanctus est psum dolor sit Lorem ipsum or sit amet, setetur sadipscing , sed diam nonumy od tempor invidunt ut labore et dolore magna aliquyam erat, sed diam voluptua. At vero eos et accusam et justo duo dolores et ea rebum. Stet clita kasd gubergren, no sea takimata sanctus est Lorem ipsum dolor sit amet.

Lorem ipsum dolor sit amet, consetetur sadipscing elitr, sed diam nonumy eirmod tempor invidunt labore et dolore magna aliquyam erat, sed diam voluptua. At vero eos et accusam et justo duo dolores et ea rebum. Stet clita kasd gubergren, no sea takimata sanctus est Lorem ipsum dolor sit amet.

Lorem ipsum dolor sit amet, consetetur sadipscing elitr, sed diam nonumy eirmod tempor invidunt ut labore et dolore magna aliquyam erat, sed diam voluptua. At vero eos et accusam et justo duo dolores et ea rebum. Stet clita kasd gubergren, no sea takimata sanctus est Lorem ipsum dolor sit amet.

Barbara Jordan

February 21, 1936 – January 17, 1996

BARBARA CHARLINE JORDAN was an American lawyer, educator, and politician who was a leader of the Civil Rights Movement. A Democrat, she was the first African American elected to the Texas Senate after Reconstruction and the first Southern African American woman elected to the United States House of Representatives. She was best known for her eloquent opening statement at the House Judiciary Committee hearings during the impeachment process against Richard Nixon and as the first African American—and the first woman—to deliver a keynote address at a Democratic National Convention.

It is said that even as a child Barbara Jordan stood out for her big, bold, booming, crisp, clear, and confident voice. It was a voice that made people sit up, stand up, and take notice.

She persevered through adversity to give voice to the voiceless and to fight for civil rights, equality, and justice.

*"If you are going to play the game properly,
you'd better know every rule."*

*"If the society today allows wrongs to go
unchallenged, the impression is created that those
wrongs have the approval of the majority."*

*"There is no obstacle in the path of young people
who are poor or members of minority groups, that
hard work and preparation cannot cure."*

*"One thing is clear to me: we as human beings must be
willing to accept people who are different from ourselves."*

CIVIL RIGHTS MOVEMENT

MAYA ANGELOU

Maya Angelou

April 4, 1928 – May 28, 2014

MAYA ANGELOU (born Marguerite Annie Johnson) was an American poet, singer, memoirist, and civil rights activist. She published seven autobiographies, three books of essays, several books of poetry, and is credited with a list of plays, movies, and television shows spanning over fifty years. She received dozens of awards and more than fifty honorary degrees. She was active in the Civil Rights Movement and worked with Martin Luther King, Jr. and Malcolm X. Her books center on themes such as racism, identity, family, and travel.

In 1968, despite having almost no experience, she wrote, produced, and narrated *Blacks, Blues, Black!*, a ten-part series of documentaries about the connection between blues music and Black Americans' African heritage.

In 1969, she wrote and published her first autobiography, *I Know Why the Caged Bird Sings*, which brought her international recognition and acclaim.

*"Do the best you can until you know better.
Then when you know better, do better."*

"If someone shows you who they really are, believe them."

---

*"While one may encounter many defeats,
one must not be defeated."*

---

*"I've learned that people will forget what you said,
people will forget what you did, but people will
never forget how you made them feel."*

CIVIL RIGHTS MOVEMENT

BARACK OBAMA

Lorem ipsum dolor sit amet, consetetur sadipscing elitr, sed diam nonumy eirmod tempor invidunt ut labore et dolore magna aliquyam erat, sed diam voluptua. At vero eos et accusam et justo duo dolores et ea rebum. Stet clita kasd gubergren, no sea takimata sanctus est Lorem ipsum dolor sit amet. Lorem ipsum dolor sit amet, consetetur sadipscing elitr, sed diam nonumy eirmod tempor invidunt ut labore et dolore magna aliquyam erat, sed diam voluptua. At vero eos et accusam et justo duo dolores et ea rebum. Stet clita kasd gubergren, no sea takimata sanctus est Lorem ipsum dolor sit amet.

Lorem ipsum dolor sit amet, consetetur sadipscing elitr, sed diam nonumy eirmod tempor invidunt ut labore et dolore magna aliquyam erat, sed diam voluptua. At vero eos et accusam et justo duo dolores et ea rebum. Stet clita kasd gubergren, no sea takimata sanctus est Lorem ipsum dolor sit amet. Lorem ipsum dolor sit amet, consetetur sadipscing elitr, sed diam nonumy eirmod tempor invidunt ut labore et dolore magna aliquyam erat, sed diam voluptua. At vero eos et accusam et justo duo dolores et ea rebum. Stet clita kasd gubergren, no sea takimata sanctus est Lorem ipsum dolor sit amet.

Lorem ipsum dolor sit amet, consetetur sadipscing elitr, sed diam nonumy eirmod tempor invidunt ut labore et dolore magna aliquyam erat, sed diam voluptua. At vero eos et accusam et justo duo dolores et ea rebum. Stet clita kasd gubergren, no sea takimata sanctus est Lorem ipsum dolor sit amet.

Former President of the US
Barack Obama

August 4, 1961 – Present

BARACK HUSSEIN OBAMA III is an American politician and attorney who served as the forty-fourth president of the United States from 2009 to 2017. A member of the Democratic Party, he was the first African American president of the United States. He served as a US senator from Illinois from 1997 to 2004 and again from 2005 to 2008.

In 2009, the Nobel Peace Prize was bestowed upon then-President Barack Hussein Obama for extraordinary efforts to strengthen international diplomacy and cooperation between peoples.

"Yes we can!"

"Now, as a nation, we don't promise equal outcomes, but we were founded on the idea everybody should have an equal opportunity to succeed. No matter who you are, what you look like, where you come from, you can make it. That's an essential promise of America. Where you start should not determine where you end up."

"My fellow Americans, we are and always will be a nation of immigrants. We were strangers once, too."

Did You Know?
Africa

- In 1862, President Abraham Lincoln signed the Emancipation Proclamation largely ending slavery in the confederate states;

- In 1866, a diamond mine was found in South Africa;

- In 1886, gold was found in South Africa;

- Europeans learning of the discovery of gold and diamonds in Africa developed new interest in Africa.

  » It was insufficient that the Europeans spent the past nearly four hundred years exploiting the human and natural resources of Africa—causing its empires to collapse and fall into an economic crisis that remains today—now they wanted to seek control over the land.

- European nations such as France, Britain, Portugal, Spain, and Belgium, being most of the European nations, which engaged in the exploitation and extrication of Africa's human and natural resources, sought to now take control of the African continent.

  » They began "Scrambling for Africa" by raiding the entire continent by force, political means, and military means, in an effort to lay claim to areas throughout Africa.

- The European nations began fighting over who had the best land. The fights intensified. There was concern about a war breaking out.

  » Concerned about the anxiety and tensions between the fighting European nations, the chancellor of Germany, Otto Von Bismarck, called a meeting of thirteen nations in Europe as well as the United States to take part in a meeting to discuss the European colonization and trade policies in Africa.

- » This meeting was called the Berlin Conference.

- The Berlin Conference was held on November 15, 1884 and continued until it closed on February 26, 1885.

  - » No African leaders were invited to participate.

  - » There were fourteen Europe nations present at this meeting, including the United States of America, namely:

    - » Germany, Austria-Hungary, Denmark, Belgium, Spain, France, the Netherlands, Italy, the United Kingdom, Portugal, Russia, Sweden, and the Ottoman Empire.

- The conference served as a forum and opportunity for the European nations to quell their animosities towards each other and a forum in which to discuss dividing up Africa so that everyone got a piece of the continent, allowing them to control, exploit, and access the resources.

- It was determined that any European nation could claim any African country by simply telling other nations that it was theirs and by showing that they could control the area claimed.

  - » This invoked racialist assumptions under the theory of social Darwinism—the white race is superior to the Black race and thus should control all of Africa.

  - » They would draw boundaries and impose their political, social, and military influence in regions throughout Africa, with no regard for the people who lived in those territories and utter disregard for the fact that many of the Africans spoke different languages and had different cultures and traditions (not that it would have justified the conduct of the Europeans).

- At the end of the conference, Africa was divided in the following manner:

> » France gained control of the northwestern part of Africa, including Algeria.

> » The British had control over both Egypt and South Africa.

> » Belgium gained control over the Congo and central Africa. Portugal gained control over the western and eastern regions of Africa.

- After World War I, this changed as Africa gained its independence.

- The impact of imperialism imposed on the African people is still being felt today, just as the impact of the institution of slavery imposed by the European nations in the Americas especially on the continent of North America, continues to have long-standing impact on the lives of African Americans today—over 146,365 days later.

Chapter 14
The Transition

---

*"The only person you are destined to become
is the person you decide to be."*

—Ralph Waldo Emerson

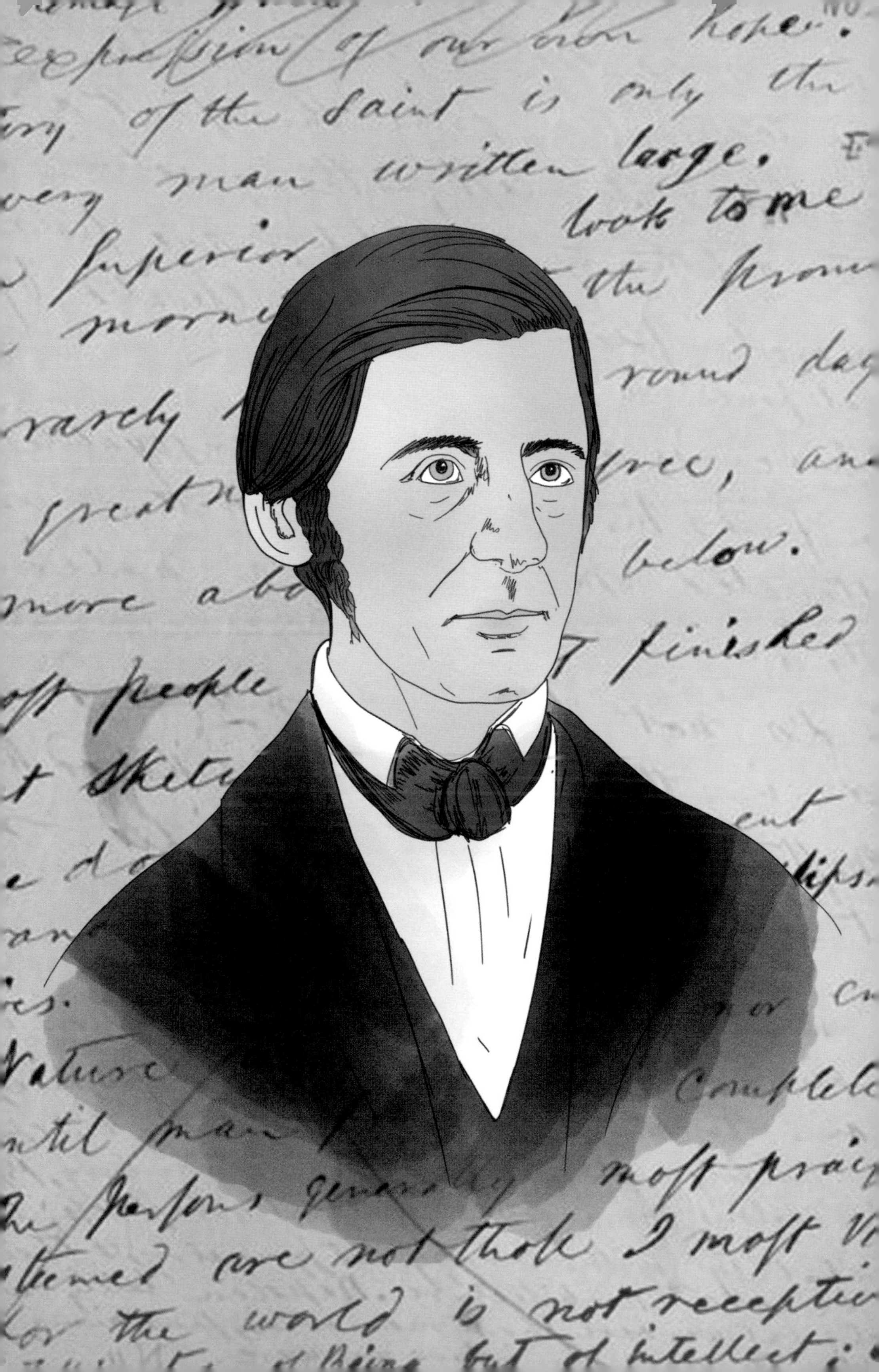

*"Be not the slave of your own past—
plunge into the sublime seas, dive deep, and swim far,
so you shall come back with new self-respect, with new
power, and with an advanced experience that shall explain and overlook the old."*

—Ralph Waldo Emerson

"So Justin, do you see why it was important to not rush through this story?" Mom asked. "Do you have a better understanding of what slavery was?"

"Yeah, I guess so!" Justin responded.

"Then my job is done—for now!"

"No, Mom. Remember, you said, 'This is a journey, not a race!' So your journey isn't over. With me around, it's just begun!"

Mom laughed. "Yes, Justin, there is always more work to be done."

"Hey, Mom," Justin said in a soft voice, "you never told me why they called people 'Black.'"

"Well, you see, son, when African Americans first arrived in the American colonies, they were called 'Africans' after the continent they came from."

Mom continued, "The oldest Black church in the United States is called the African Methodist Episcopal Church. Later, the descendants of the African diaspora here to North America were referred to as 'colored people.'

"The nation's oldest civil rights group is called the National Association for the Advancement of Colored People, or the NAACP. Bet you didn't know that, huh?"

"Of course I don't know what that means. I'm just a kid—those were names of places in the old days, when…"

Hearing the sarcasm in his voice, Mom bent down to look Justin right in the eyes. "Go ahead. What were you going to say? Old days, when...what?"

"Uh, the old days when they called people colored people?"

"Good answer. I know you, Mister..."

Justin snuck in a laugh as he tried to get out of the hammock.

"Later on, African Americans were referred to as Negroes. In 1914, the political leader Marcus Garvey founded a group called the United Negro Improvement Association, or UNIA.

"During the 1960s, the reference to 'Black' replaced the word 'Negro' as the common term. An example of a group that uses that designation is the Congressional Black Caucus.

"And today, 'African American' is the preferred term—reflecting both the group's African origins and its members' status as American citizens.

"Discrimination exists against several groups in America, like:

- African Americans
- Asian Americans
- Latin Americans
- Native Americans

"My goal is to preserve your identity and self-esteem, and remind you every step of the way that you have a voice in this world. I encourage you to find your VIP status—your Voice, Identity, and Purpose—and don't be afraid to use it thoughtfully and with a purpose!"

Chapter 15

Remembering What the Phenomenal People with Phenomenal Stories Shared with You!

"Phenomenal People with Phenomenal Stories—
creating diversity of voice, vision, and purpose
for children as they receive the social and emotional
benefits that should come with an education."

—Deidra R. Moore-Janvier, Esq.

"So beloved, as we grow older and are blessed with life, I want you to always remember this quote from Ralph Waldo Emerson:

To laugh often and much;
To win the respect of intelligent people
and the affection of children;
To earn the appreciation of honest critics
and endure the betrayal of false friends;
To appreciate beauty, to find the best in others;
To leave the world a bit better,
whether by a healthy child, a garden patch,
or a redeemed social condition;
To know even one life has breathed
easier because you have lived.
That is to have succeeded.

"And always remember what the presenters of the Phenomenal People with Phenomenal Stories speaker series shared with you and the K–5 students at your school during the 2018-2020 academic year.

DR. ONEEKA WILLIAMS

Remember what Dr. Oneeka Williams, the urologic surgeon and award-winning author told you in October 2019…

When she visited your school on two separate occasions and introduced you and your schoolmates to her *Dr. Dee Dee Dynamo's* book series, *Not Even the Sky is the Limit!*

'Not Even the Sky is the Limit!'

PAMELA C.V. JOLLY

Remember what Pamela C.V. Jolly shared at the
Parents of Color committee meeting in November 2019:

Our History

Our history plays an important part in seeding one's pursuit of life purpose, which can lead to legacy wealth. As benefactors of history, we have a unique shared narrative from which to pull. Understanding the history that came before you, specifically the decisions that led to where we are today in society, plays an important role in framing the picture we are posing for together. This macro view invites the individual to fully participate in the collective group process we are all navigating together.

Elders   **Adults**   **Youth**   **Tribe**

Pamela C.V. Jolly is the founder and CEO of Torch Enterprises, Inc. She is a nationally and internationally sought after speaker, lecturing and advising businesses and leaders with her research and work in places such as Korea, China, Japan, Africa, the Caribbean, and most recently Oxford, England.

EDWIDGE DANTICAT

Remember what Edwidge Danticat told you
and your classmates in September 2019,
when she quoted Toni Morrison:

> *"If there is a book that you want to read, but it hasn't been written yet, then you must write it."*

—Toni Morrison

Danticat was born in Port-au-Prince, Haiti. When she was two years old, her father immigrated to New York, to be followed two years later by her mother. Danticat began writing at nine years old.

In 1993, she earned a master of fine arts in creative writing from Brown University. Her thesis, titled "My Turn in the Fire—An Abridged Novel," was the basis for her novel *Breath, Eyes, Memory,* which was published by Soho Press in 1994. Four years later, it became an Oprah's Book Club selection.

CALVIN HILL

And lastly, remember the advice the legendary Calvin Hill shared with us:

"Knowledge of one's history creates a platform to successfully engage the present and the future!"

Calvin G. Hill is a retired American football player. He played running back in the National Football League for twelve seasons. Hill played for the Dallas Cowboys, Washington Football team, and Cleveland Browns. He also played a season with the Hawaiians of the World Football League in 1975.

IN ORDER TO KNOW WHERE YOU ARE GOING...

...YOU MUST KNOW WHERE YOU COME FROM!

"My son was around your age when he asked me, "What is slavery?" And that is when I decided to have a child-appropriate conversation about our history…

You must know where
you come from …
in order to know
where you are going!

...the history of African Americans in America! And that's the story of *From Me to You: The Power of Storytelling and Its Inherent Generational Wealth—An African American Story!*"

My parents are proud of me!

My family and friends
love me for who I am!

I approve of myself!

I fully ACCEPT myself and know that
I am WORTHY of GREAT things in LIFE!

I FOCUS ON SOLUTIONS
AND ALWAYS FIND THE BEST ONE!

I AM SPECIAL!

I BELIEVE I CAN BE
WHATEVER I WANT TO BE!

My personality exudes confidence!

I am in charge of my own life!

I DRAW INSPIRATION FROM LIFE
AND MY ROLE MODELS!

I listen to my parents and respect them!

I love going to school
because learning is fun!

I have fears, but I have
the courage to face them!

I believe in myself!

I am helpful, courageous,
generous, and grateful!

"Those who are not looking for happiness are most likely to find it, because those who are searching forget that the surest way to be happy is to seek happiness for others!"

—Dr. Martin Luther King, Jr.

A place for *you* to write *your* own
affirmations, dreams, and goals!

A Message From the Author

- From 1619 – 1865, enslaved Africans were treated as chattels, while white Americans deprived them of their lives physically, mentally, and emotionally. White Americans robbed African Americans of their life, liberty, and ultimately the pursuit of happiness while forcing them to live in slavery for 246 years.

- From 1865 – 1965, although African Americans had certain rights and privileges under the Thirteenth, Fourteenth, and Fifteenth Amendments—rights and privileges that were ratified, respectively, in 1865, 1868, and 1870—white Americans, through the use of repressive and oppressive laws such as the Black Codes and Jim Crow laws, continued the practice of exploiting and oppressing the life of the African American man, woman, and child. However, this form of exploitative conduct by white Americans came in the form of racial segregation, terroristic acts by white supremacists (such as the Ku Klux Klan), and psychological warfare by using lynching to set examples of what would happen to an African American if they attempted to vote, educate themselves, create a community, or try in any way to make a life for themselves.

» During the one hundred years that followed the abolishment of slavery, African Americans gained little from the labor force that, again, robbed them of sweat equity, entrepreneurship, home-ownership, education, income, and an ability to create and attain wealth. They were particularly robbed of their share in the multibillion dollar industry that was established at the expense of the African American's freedom—freedom from being enslaved physically, mentally, and emotionally—by being forced into servitude again for the next one hundred years.

• African Americans have suffered greatly from the long-enduring effects of slavery in America after having endured centuries of discriminatory, repressive, and gut-wrenching laws and practices.

More than four hundred years later, African Americans remain a marginalized group in the United States, notwithstanding the many, many contributions in all facets of American culture. The institution of slavery afforded Europeans, and by extension others, the opportunity to create wealth and power at the expense of African Americans.

In the end, it is important to know that African Americans have spent more than four hundred years trying to get America to honor that part of the Constitution that says, "all men are created equal."

Now is the time to have an honest and productive conversation about the situation of African Americans and find a productive way to rebuild that unique form of government that I spoke of earlier. We need to rebuild the government in which the government, laws, judicial system, educational system, housing system, political system, and all the resources and privileges afforded people in America only applied to those of the European background are reconstructed in a way that ensures any one or all of the below:

- African Americans receive relief in the form of financial payments—just as the federal government has provided financial relief to Japanese Americans for the atrocities committed on them—during the internment of Japanese Americans in the United States during World War II—led to forced relocation and incarceration in concentration camps.

- The establishment of a governmental agency much like the Freedmen's Bureau that was enacted by President Abraham Lincoln on March 3, 1865, as a part of the US Department of War, which was intended, partly, to assist and provide aid for the four million recently free slaves.

- The creation or reinstatement of an act similar to the Homestead Act, which was enacted by President Abraham Lincoln on May 20, 1862, granting Americans 160-acre plots of public land for the price of a small filing fee.

  » Citing from an article written by History.com editors, "Homestead Act," it provides President Abraham Lincoln's explanation as to why the Homestead Act was passed.

  » "In a July 4, 1861 speech, Lincoln told the nation the purpose of America's government was "to elevate the condition of men, to lift artificial burdens from all shoulders, and to give everyone an unfettered start and a fair chance in the race of life." As the author goes on to say, "He followed through with the passage of the Homestead Act, which remained active for 124 years until it was repealed in 1976, and resulted in 10 percent of US land—or 270 million acres—to be claimed and settled."[29]

» The author goes on to say: "In 1976, the Homestead Act was repealed with the passage of the federal Land Policy and Management Act, which states that 'public lands be retained in federal ownership.' The Act authorizes the US Bureau of Land Management to manage federal lands. Homesteading was still allowed for another decade in Alaska, until 1986."[29]

- What better way to show good faith by the federal government than to assist African Americans in the free flow of information, in an unequivocal and clear manner, as to how to gain access to and how to secure access to the billions of acres of land currently managed by the federal government, thus affording African Americans an opportunity to build communities and increase wealth ownership throughout parts of the United States. African Americans never received the "forty acres and a mule," that was promised to the freedmen by the federal government, at the end of the Civil War.

- African Americans secure reparations for the catastrophic upheaval of forcibly removing African Americans from their homeland of Africa to the United States—just as Jewish Americans received reparations from the federal government as a result of the Holocaust that happened upon their communities, which impacted our fellow Americans as descendants of the Holocaust; and

- African Americans gain access to the treaties—much like those put in place for the Native Americans—Indian Treaties, which grant the Natives at least three billion dollars annually and which help protect and preserve their common welfare in their communities.

African Americans have generated trillions of dollars for this country by providing the "free labor" that came as a result of the institution of slavery, where African Americans were for more than 246 years enslaved Africans treated as chattel under institutionalized slavery; and during the one hundred years that followed the abolition of slavery—with the resulting "forced labor" that kept African Americans in servitude. However, today, as in the land of wealth and opportunity in 1863, African Americans have one-half of one percent of the nation's wealth! This premise is *unremarkable! Inequitable! And unconscionable!*

It is time to push for equity from our government, to redress the exploitation of African Americans for more than four hundred years—in a country where the blood, sweat, tears, and lives lost contributed to the creation, development, and sustainability of this country and created wealth and opportunity for many others; but we must also push to educate and inform our children—and by extension, the world—as to the oppressive treatment of African Americans in this country.

My hope is that you will glean from these pages an understanding and clarity about racism in America, specifically the extent of the oppression that has plagued the African American culture since the forming of our imperfect nation—more than four hundred years ago![29]

This is *From Me to You: The Power of Storytelling and Its Inherent Generational Wealth— An African American Story!*

—Deidra R. Moore-Janvier, Esq.

Acknowledgments

Writing a book is more challenging than I thought and more fulfilling and gratifying than I could have ever imagined. None of this would have been possible without finding hope, faith, courage, and inspiration from various people during the seasons of my life.

I want to thank my ancestors for leaving a legacy of courage, strength, resilience, and optimism, as you gave your blood, sweat, tears, and lives lost in the fight for freedom from the forced bondage of our people. The legacy of character strengths exhibited by the tens of millions of enslaved Africans and their descendants—even during the most egregious times of their lives—will always be honored and cherished by the children of the world today and for generations to come.

I want to thank my late maternal grandmother, Loretta, who influenced my life, for the courage she exhibited when, shortly after the death of her husband—my grandfather—Benjamin (who died in 1954), she, wanting a better life for her six children with more opportunities afforded to her than during the Jim Crow era of the South migrated from Charleston, South Carolina, to New York. This would be the beginning of her plans for a new life for her and her children in New York.

I thank her for reinforcing the value of an education and being an inspiration when she, at the age of fifty, enrolled in and completed a college degree at the College of New Rochelle.

I want to thank my late mother, Marie, for giving me life and for showing courage in the decisions she made that were in the best interests of her family, particularly when needing to love me differently. I've learned over the years that you did the best you could with what you had, and for that I am eternally grateful.

I want to thank my father, Walter, for giving me life and for teaching me the value in forgiveness, understanding, and maintaining family connections where possible.

I want to thank my maternal aunt Virginia for being a constant in my life and loving me unconditionally.

I want to thank my husband, Pierre, for journeying this life with me for the past 4,881 days and counting, but thank you most of all for providing your unwavering love and support during the process of writing this book.

To my daughter, thank you for enduring the sacrifices that come with making a difference in the lives of others—always remember: "I love you to infinity—and beyond!"

To my son, thank you for being the inspiration behind this book! Always remember: "I love you to infinity—and beyond!" You and "Sis" are my proudest achievements!

I am eternally grateful to my dear friend, Peter M. Jordan, who for the past thirty-three years has not only watched me grow and follow my dreams, but who has also played a major role in my life when it came to my decisions to take risks. He encouraged and showed full support of me and the decisions I made. When I became a single mother to my daughter, he was supportive of the decisions I made as I planned a life for us; when I purchased my first home at the age of twenty-five, he encouraged me; when I quit my job at TIAA-CREF after nine years of full-time employment to attend law school full-time, he was supportive of my decision; when I had to work three jobs while in law school to meet the demands of being a single mom, he encouraged me; when I found true love in my husband, Pierre Michel Janvier, it was Peter Michael Jordan who encouraged me (note the shared initials). For the past thirty-three years, as my life was filled with many ups and downs, Peter was that constant in my life—one who never tried to stop me but who always encouraged me.

I want to thank my dearest friend Miranda Blake Melhalf for her incredible heart and, as in all things, her invaluable support. She stood by me during every struggle and all my successes. That is true friendship.

I want to thank my dearest friend Martine Nicolas for sustaining me with her friendship for more than thirty years, since our time at TIAA-CREF. Thank you for reminding me that there is something valuable to share with the content of this book.

A special thank you to the leader of Riverdale Country School, Dominic A.A. Randolph, head of school, and your administration: Kelley Nicholson-Flynn (former head of upper school), Milton Sipp (head of middle school), Sandy S. Shaller (former head of lower school), and Dr. James Duval (current head of lower school). Your commitment (and that of your respective teams) to fostering a diverse, equitable, and inclusive environment at the Riverdale Country School is to be applauded. I found inspiration in your leadership and your commitment to diversity, equity, inclusion, and belonging.

An especially heartfelt thank you to those Phenomenal People with Phenomenal Stories who shared their journeys with our youth during my leadership at Riverdale Country School as chair of the Parents of Color Committee during the

2018–2020 academic school year. Thank you to Dr. Oneeka Williams, Edwidge Danticat, Dr. Pamela C.V. Jolly, Dr. Jeffrey Gardere, and the legendary retired NFL Player Calvin Hill. I thank everyone for allowing illustrations and personal messages to be included in this book.

I am grateful to the team at Mascot Books, who helped bring my vision to life. A special thank you to Naren Aryal, CEO and publisher of Mascot Books, and Kate McDaniel, who, on March 12, 2020, read the manuscript, listened to my vision for the book, and offered me my first book deal on March 20, 2020.

I want to extend special thanks to those people who consistently provided words of encouragement at times when they didn't know I needed it, particularly during those periods of self-doubt, setbacks, and uncertainty that I now know are a part of the daunting yet beautiful process of writing a book: Oneeka W., Edwidge D., Ryon M., Lynn B., Elena J., Patricia G., Jean M., Veronica C., Jessica D., Desiree T., Reginald A., Janet H., Mieasia E., Rachel D., and my cousin Carol Holmes.

Lastly, a special thank you to my illustrator, Valerie Bouthyette—your exquisite illustrations make *From Me to You: The Power of Storytelling and Its Inherent Generational Wealth—An African American Story* that much more enjoyable to read.

Notes

1   "Othering the Slave Owner," *American Slavery, American Imperialism*, Cambridge University Press, pp. 107–146, August 31, 2020.

2   Alexander, J. (2001). "Islam, Archaeology, and Slavery in Africa." *World Archaeology*. 33 (1): 44–60.

3   Ochieng' William Robert (1975). *Eastern Kenya and Its Invaders*. East African Literature Bureau, p. 76. Retrieved May 15, 2015.

4   Bethwell A. Ogot, *Zamani: A Survey of East African History* (East African Publishing House: 1974), p. 104.

5   Spyropoulos, Yannis, "Slaves and Freedmen" in 17th – and Early 18th – Century Ottoman Crete, *Turcica*, 46, 2015, p. 181, 182.

6   Yeager, Timothy J. *"Encomienda or Slavery? The Spanish Crown's Choice of Labor Organization in Sixteenth-Century Spanish America."*

7   Lovejoy, Paul E. (2012). *"Transformations in Slavery: A History of Slavery in Africa."* London: Cambridge University Press.

8   Painter, Neil Irvin; Berlin, Ira (2000). *"Many Thousands Gone: The First Two Centuries of Slavery in North America."* African American Review. 34 (3): 515.

9   Noel King (ed.), *Ibn Battuta in Black Africa*, Princeton 2005, p. 54.

10 Fage, J. D. (1969). *"Slavery and the Slave Trade in the Context of West African History."* The Journal of African History. 10 (3) 393–404.

11 Rodney, Walker (1966), *"African Slavery and Other Forms of Social Oppression on the Upper Guinea Coast in the Context of the Atlantic Slave-Trade."* The Journal of African History. 7 (3): 431–443.

12 Wigington, Patti. *"African Americans in the Revolutionary War."* ThoughtCo. https://www.thoughtco.com (accessed October 15, 2020).

13 Evan Andrews, "7 Famous Slave Revolts," *History Stories*. Updated January 18, 2019 (Originally published January 15, 2013).

14 Wigington, Patti. *"African Americans in the Revolutionary War."* ThoughtCo. https://www.thoughtco.com/African Americans-in-the-revolutionary-war-4151706 (accessed October 15, 2020).

15 Andrews, Evan. "How Many US Presidents Owned Enslaved People?" History.com. AETN Networks. July 19, 2017. https://www.history.com/news/how-many-u-s-presidents-owned-slaves (accessed September 3, 2019).

16 Urofsky, Melvin I. "Dred Scott Decision," *Encyclopedia Britannica*. www.britannica.com/event/Dred-Scott-decision. October 18, 2020.

17 Eric Foner, *Unfinished Revolution* 1863–1877 (New York: Harper & Row, 1988).

18 David Herbert Donald, Jean Baker, and Michael Holt, *Civil War & Reconstruction* (New York: Norton, 2001).

19 *Lynchburg Daily Virginian*, March 1, 2, 4, 5, 1867.

20 *Montgomery Daily Advertiser*, March 16, 1867.

21 David Herbert Donald, Jean Baker, and Michael Holt, *Civil War & Reconstruction* (New York: Norton, 2001).

22 Eric Foner, *Unfinished Revolution* 1863–1877 (New York: Harper & Row, 1988).

23 *Lynchburg Daily Virginian*, March 22, 1867.

24 *Montgomery Daily Advertiser*, March 16, 1867.

25 Eric Foner, *Reconstruction America's Unfinished Revolution*, 1863–1877 (New York: Harper & Row Publishers, 1988).

26 *National Intelligencer*, July 19, 1867.

27 "The President's Veto Message," *Daily Dispatch*, July 22, 1867.

28 Nittle, Nandra Kareem. "How the Black Codes Limited African American Progress After the Civil War." History.com. AETN Networks. October 1, 2020. https://www.history.com/news/black-codes-reconstruction-slavery.

29 "Homestead Act," History.com. Published November 9, 2009. (Accessed October 20, 2020).

30 Butler, Nic. *"The End of the Trans-Atlantic Slave Trade."* Charleston County Public Library, January 26, 2018.

31 Wise, Warren L. *"350 years ago, Charleston's first settlers carved a new colony in a pristine wilderness." The Post and Courier.* April 17, 2020; Updated Dec 29, 2020.